PENGUIN BOOKS
BEYOND STORMS AND STARS

Noeleen Heyzer was an Under-Secretary-General of the United Nations and the highest ranking Singaporean in the United Nations (2007–2015). She was the first woman to serve as the Executive Secretary of the UN Economic and Social Commission for Asia and the Pacific since its founding in 1947. Under her leadership (2007-2014), the commission focused on regional cooperation for a more resilient Asia-Pacific, founded on shared prosperity, social equity, and sustainable development. She was at the forefront of many innovations including for regional disaster preparedness, inclusive socio-economic policies, sustainable agriculture and urbanization, energy security and regional connectivity.

She was the first Executive Director from outside North America to lead the United Nations Development Fund for Women (1994-2007). She was widely recognized for her pivotal role in the Security Council's formulation and implementation of the landmark Resolution 1325 on Women, Peace, and Security, and undertook extensive missions to conflict-affected countries worldwide. She was also the UNSG's Special Adviser for Timor-Leste, working to support peace-building, state-building, and sustainable development.

She holds a BA (Upper Hons) and a MSc from Singapore University, a PhD from Cambridge University, and has received numerous international awards for leadership including the Dag Hammarskjöld Medal (2004).

T0148824

This is a remarkable book by a remarkable person which deserves to be read by all those interested in development issues and international affairs. The book shows Noeleen Heyzer's inspiring journey, made possible by her vibrant personality that combined pioneering leadership with the zeal to build a better and fairer world. The book gives insights into the inner workings of the UN system and shows it is possible to make its agencies work for the betterment of humanity, if only leaders of calibre are in place and given the opportunity. Noeleen's story is a beacon of hope in our present crisis-prone world.

—Martin Khor
Executive Director, The South Centre, Geneva (2009-2018)
Founding Director, Third World Network

BEYOND STORMS AND STARS

A MEMOIR

NOELEEN HEYZER

PENGUIN BOOKS
An imprint of Penguin Random House

PENGUIN BOOKS

USA | Canada | UK | Ireland | Australia
New Zealand | India | South Africa | China | Southeast Asia

Penguin Books is part of the Penguin Random House group of companies
whose addresses can be found at global.penguinrandomhouse.com

Published by Penguin Random House SEA Pte Ltd
9, Changi South Street 3, Level 08-01,
Singapore 486361

First published in Penguin Books by Penguin Random House SEA 2021

10 9 8 7 6 5 4 3 2 1

ISBN 9789814954242

Typeset in Adobe Garamond Pro by Manipal Technologies Limited, Manipal

www.penguin.sg

In memory of my mother
and
for my daughters,
Lilianne and Pauline

Contents

Foreword

Amartya Sen

I am honoured—and touched—by the admirable Noeleen Heyzer's kind request to read her memoir and offer my comments. The book is a splendid account of her life, seen from her own perspective.

From the difficult and deprived days of Noeleen's childhood (with serious, if intermittent, poverty and persistent uncertainty), we move with her through her elevating educational years—including her training at the National University of Singapore and her encounter with the traditions of Cambridge University—and then share the powerful experiences of her productive, and ultimately stellar, professional life. I found it particularly striking to get an understanding of the way Noeleen takes care to establish a firm grip on her surroundings at every stage of her life— from her somewhat precarious childhood to the period of her well-known leadership of important international initiatives in the global world. If her modesty leads her to an understatement of the commanding role she has had in the advancement of gender justice and in contributing to Asia's resurgence in the

modern world, she does share with us how each stage of her life
has helped her to move to the next.

The book is immensely readable as an absorbing story of the
life of one of the leading women in the modern world, but it is
also much more than that. It is, first of all, a recollection of an
indomitable urge to overcome the disadvantages of childhood to
create a life for oneself. Noeleen's life brings out how a reflected
resolve can make a big difference to the way one's life unfolds—
overcoming initial handicaps.

Second, the account of Noeleen's life is a strong vindication
of the transformative role of education, which, in her case,
begins in the schooling she managed to get—with her
grandmother's help—in her otherwise deprived childhood.
Then we see her through her college days in Singapore and
Cambridge. Noeleen's strong ingenious spirit is, of course, an
important factor in her remarkable social mobility; but, as a
major instrument of change, education does play a big part in
her evolving life.

Finally, there is an implicit tribute here to the productivity
of institutions in the way Noeleen's professional life achieves
outstanding success. Noeleen's exceptional skills and talents
become powerfully constructive in making excellent use of the
two institutions of the United Nations (UN) that she successively
leads—the Development Fund for Women (UNIFEM) and
the Economic and Social Commission for Asia and the Pacific
(ESCAP). There is a huge complementarity there between
the potentialities of international institutions and the reality
of Noeleen's leadership abilities, with her values, competence,
and imagination.

This is a great book for the understanding it offers as well as the enjoyment we get from reading it. I end by congratulating Noeleen Heyzer for an excellent contribution.

Professor Amartya Sen
Nobel Laureate in Economics (1998)
Professor of Economics and Philosophy,
Harvard University (present)
Master of Trinity College,
University of Cambridge (1998–2004)
Professor of Economics, Nuffield College,
University of Oxford (1977–88)

Foreword

Richard Jolly

This is a book for those who want to make a positive difference in the world. It is the true story of how serious change can happen or be made to happen in different parts of the world, even from very difficult beginnings and when opposed by powerful interests. The book is one of the best memoirs I have read in recent times. It is an inspiration for vision, determination, and persistence for women, and men, including all those juggling with the pressures of time in bringing up children or caring for others while working full-time, as well as for those with more time and less pressure.

The book is important and deserves to be read from the first page to the last. It's a vivid story, brilliantly written, with heart-wrenching moments as well as joyful achievements and successes. Even those who are short on time should read important sections which can help and inspire them to take action.

Feminists of any gender might want to start with Chapter 4, academics and researchers might start with Chapter 3, and students and teachers with Chapter 2.

Those who have had a difficult childhood, which they feel is still holding them back, should start at the beginning. Those working internationally in the UN or elsewhere need to read all of chapters 5, 6, 7, and 8. These will be especially helpful to those in leadership positions, or who are short on financial resources or facing other obstacles.

Chapter 7 should probably be read by everyone, but especially by men. It is harrowing even to read a vivid description of how rape is, and has been, used in war and conflict. It brings out the evil tragedies, women's brave witness, early failures to recognize and criminalize the impact of war on women and, eventually, the groundbreaking achievement in the UN Security Council. As painful as the reality of rape is, this chapter also offers hope in demonstrating how women can, and must, be brought into conflict resolution and actions towards sustaining peace. In a world still torn by conflicts in every continent, all of us need to read this chapter, and understand and press for implementing its basic lessons.

Noeleen Heyzer started her career as a student political activist, then became an academic researcher and, eventually, a global leader at the UN—always passionate to empower women, especially those in marginalized situations and communities.

She grew up in the dying days of colonialism when the struggle for citizens of newly independent nations was to build their new societies and politics with idealism and vision. As she writes, 'It was our political awakening. We asked ourselves: What was the right path for Singapore—democracy, socialism, capitalism, or a creative combination of all? Not theoretical, but real choices.'

She combined all this with motherhood, learning to juggle the competing demands of children and work while never losing sight of the vision for progress in the long run.

The book contains important lessons for anyone working in a bureaucracy: How to raise doubts about the reasons given for inaction or how to check and then challenge the reasons given, or why bolder actions must be ruled out. Noeleen shows how action can be taken in different situations.

Academics can learn a lot from her struggles to make research count—for instance, by mobilizing victims to explain their situations and lead the actions required for change. Noeleen's research into deforestation in the Limbang region of Sarawak is especially revealing. The state government had put the blame on shifting cultivation rather than on those involved in logging or cutting the forests to make way for oil palm plantations. Noeleen's research not only revealed the truth but also identified a way forward which mobilized political support—by moving to a situation of joint land titles where women as well as men could own land.

The lessons on leadership in the UN strike me with great force and relevance. I found myself literally cheering out loud while reading Chapter 5, as the financial cutbacks and compromises offered were one by one rejected and then overcome. And, in the previous chapter, there are lessons on how to resist corruption within the UN itself. It is a rare story, but vital, full of lessons on political, national and international issues.

Noeleen had an extraordinary early life—poverty, hunger mixed with charity, education, a deeply caring uncle, and a wonderful grandmother who believed that the only way out for a girl was education and to develop a 'strong brain'. Noeleen followed the advice, escaping her early obstacles and developing a 'strong brain' and a most determined character—not leaving her background behind, but building from it with determination to change such obstacles for others growing up in disadvantaged circumstances. Her whole life, and this book, is born out of struggle, leading to ultimate triumph. It's an important story.

Sir Richard Jolly
Honorary Professor, Institute of Development
Studies (IDS), University of Sussex (present)
Executive Director, Institute of
Development Studies, University of Sussex (1972–81)
Deputy Executive Director, United Nations
Children Fund (UNICEF) (1982–95)
Director and lead author,
Human Development Report
1995–2000, United Nations
Development Programme (UNDP)

Author's Preface

None of us chooses the time and place we are born in. I was born in Singapore a few years after the end of the Second World War—a moment of history marked by political upheaval and social transition. As with all endings, it was a time of beginnings too—the end of colonialism and imperialism heralded the birth of new nations across Asia and the world, promising a better life for its people. I came into the world during these turbulent times; perhaps this is why I have always had the sense of 'coming of age' alongside my country as it struggled for freedom to chart its own destiny.

As I tried to make sense of my own community, and the circumstances I found myself in as a young woman, I discovered that many women and men were grappling with their own circumstances, attempting to envision and shape the future of their society. Growing up in post-war Singapore, I became acutely aware of a combination of disruptive and volatile forces that left human beings vulnerable—ideological contestations, political and economic instability, social inequality, and racial and gender discrimination. Yet, I also witnessed the resilience of the human spirit, how people found their own strength—individually and collectively—to engage, negotiate, and reshape the forces that impacted their lives. I understood that vulnerable people are never merely victims, and that people possess a vital agency of thought and action to respond to even the most difficult circumstances. People have the power to come together, initiate change, and cocreate new possibilities.

This book is a reflection on my life's journey—from my early years in Singapore to my intellectual development at the University of Cambridge and the IDS at the University of Sussex, to my work in gender and development at the Asia Pacific Development Centre, and to my years at the UN. In the process of writing, it became clear to me that many of my life choices have been urged by my belief in the power of people to shape their own lives and define their own destinies despite the larger than life forces that seem to be beyond their control. The storms that wreaked havoc on my childhood ignited a great resolve within me to defy what was 'written in the stars' of my destiny. I was determined to change my life. In the midst of the deprivation and discrimination that surrounded me, I dared to imagine a different world.

Throughout my life, my innate spirit of resistance has been one of my deepest strengths. I have refused to accept social injustice as a norm and resisted systems of oppression in all forms, convinced that we must break these barriers to revitalize our societies, rejuvenate ourselves, and recreate relationships anew. In my research and work, I discovered a legacy of courage of others who have come before me, of women engaged in the thought and practice of transforming their societies. This legacy of ideas and activism has inspired and guided me in my work on empowering women to change structures of discrimination that thrive on vulnerability and inequality. Yet, I have found that even lines of resistance need to be constantly reimagined and redrawn, that no one can define your struggle or vision of change, and that each of us must forge our own path as a solitary stream in the landscape of our history before we come together as a confluence that opens to a powerful sea.

Finally, I have sought out spaces in institutions that allow me to wield power as a vehicle for transformation and empowerment to create social arrangements that promote greater fairness and dignity. In my leadership roles at the UN, focusing on issues such as women's economic security and rights, ending violence against women (VAW), and bringing women to the peace table, I have tried to embody a different kind of global leadership—where power resonates from deep experience rather than privilege and can be effectively harnessed to empower vulnerable communities. I have learnt that multilateral organizations and global institutions are not fixed structures that are disconnected from real life; they are made up of living, breathing human beings who belong to an ever-evolving world. We should, therefore, strive to create our institutions not as rigid bureaucracies, but as organic ecosystems that help us realize and enact our collective vision of idealism, hope, and humanity.

Noeleen Heyzer

1

Dark Days, New Dawn

'If we do not know our own history, we are doomed to live it as though it were our private fate.'

—*Hannah Arendt*

Life has a way of revealing its paradoxes through the drama of despair and hope that it plays out in each of our realities. From an early age, I became aware that my life was connected to the ebb and flow of history and the shifting contours of a society at the threshold of nationhood.

I was born in Singapore three years after the end of the Second World War. It was a time of upheaval—the world still bore the fresh wounds of war as it witnessed the decline of imperialist power and the rise of nationalism in the colonies. Before the war, Singapore had been one of three port cities, with Malacca and Penang, along the Strait of Malacca that came under British control and were collectively known as the Straits Settlements. After the war, Singapore became a separate British Crown Colony. An important entrepôt strategically located at the crossroads of flourishing international trade, Singapore drew migrant workers in droves from China, India and beyond. There were bonded workers and people who were escaping poverty and famine, mainly from China. There were those fleeing the disintegration of their societies, including families escaping the violent Hindu–Muslim partition of British India. And there were those who had come to Singapore looking for new opportunities—entrepreneurs from South China; merchants of Arab, Indian, Armenian, and Jewish descent; traders from the Malay Archipelago; missionaries and educators from Ireland and France. My own ancestors were among these migrants who had come to Singapore in search of a brighter future.

I come from a confluence of two vastly different streams of people. My mother's stream traces its source to Fujian province in southern China. I do not know when my Chinese ancestors arrived on the shores of Singapore. For me, the person who linked the family's distant origins to the living present was my grandmother—the most perennial and powerful figure of my childhood. One of my earliest memories was of grandma carrying me on her back by the sea, to let me breathe in the morning air which she believed would heal my whooping cough. I was around three years old at the time. Grandma would wake me at the crack of dawn, sling me over her small, bent back and walk to the sea along the East Coast, about a mile away from our kampong house in Telok Kurau. I was soothed by the rhythm of her movement as she walked. I took in the sound of the waves and the early light from the sky, and felt the sea breeze open up my breathing. I later learned that grandma, who carried me, carried many secrets and stories with her, too.

My grandmother's story is not unlike those of so many girls at that time in colonial Singapore. She was adopted, very likely as a mui tsai[1], a girl who was brought in to serve in a family. This was a time when people were escaping the feudal–patriarchal society in China. Young women and girls were running away from child

---

[1]   *Tsai* means young, *mui* means girl.

marriages and discrimination in both rural and urban families. In Singapore, many poor families still sold their daughters or gave them away as mui tsai, many of whom became 'live-in servants'. Faced with grinding poverty, the alternative to selling or adoption was to abandon newborn girls. Consequently, unwanted newborn girls were left as orphans at the doorsteps of the Victoria Street Convent of the Holy Infant Jesus—a school and orphanage for girls set up by Catholic nuns—or in rubbish bins to die. Polygamy and keeping concubines were also common practices. Many women and girls were easily discarded, left in distressful and vulnerable situations with no legal rights and protection. This was the reality of colonial Singapore in which my grandmother grew up.

Grandma had been adopted as a child into a Peranakan[2] family, where she helped with household chores and responsibilities. It was here that she picked up the Peranakan way of speaking—a colloquial blend of Malay and Hokkien—as well as the distinctive Peranakan recipes that she later passed down in her own family, and eventually to me. During the war, grandma had to raise four children as a single mother, following the early death of her husband. She had to put one daughter up for adoption and place two others, including my mother, in the orphanage so that she could work. My grandma converted to Catholicism to secure places in mission schools so that her children would have a decent education and a life that was better than hers. Grandma had to hide her only son during the Japanese occupation because many young Chinese men and boys were being executed, as the Sino-Japanese war spilled over their borders and played itself out in South East Asia. She sent her son away with a trusted Tamil

---

[2] Peranakan refers to the Straits Chinese of Malaya (particularly in Melaka, Penang, and Singapore), the Dutch East Indies, and southern Thailand. Peranakan families are descendants of early Chinese immigrants who intermarried with local Malay communities and adopted aspects of Malay language and customs.

friend to the Raffles Lighthouse for six months. She cut off all
contact with him and waited until it was safe to bring him back
again. My grandma's life was one of courage and perseverance; she
struggled against the forces of fate and history to create a future
for her children.

The stream of my father's family traces its course back to the
German–Dutch entrepreneurs who lived for many generations in
Ceylon (now Sri Lanka) and were identified as the Dutch Burghers.
His great ancestors had arrived on the shores of Ceylon sometime
in the early eighteenth century. There were many intermarriages
among the Dutch, Anglo, and Ceylonese communities, and
eventually my grandfather migrated to Calcutta (now Kolkata) in
India, where he worked in the British civil service. My father was
born and raised in Calcutta, where he was trained in homeopathy,
traditional healing practices and, later, basic Western medicine.
Since the late nineteenth century, Calcutta had been a centre
for homoeopathic medicine, which was practised by civic and
military amateurs. During the Second World War, my father left
home to serve as a medic in the British Army in Burma and later
in Singapore.

According to family stories, my parents met while my father
was attending to the wounded in an army hospital and my mother
was working as a secretary in the army base in Seletar, Singapore.
During the war and the immediate post-war years, having certified
qualifications was not a prerequisite for a job; people were recruited
for their experience and acquired skills. During the war, whatever
skills a person had that could deal with the wounds and trauma of
conflict were in great demand and quickly put to use. But, soon
after the war and with the closure of the army hospital, proper
paper certification became necessary to establish a clinic with the
legalization of professional skills. My father was made redundant,
and he could not legally establish his practice—and the family fell

into deep poverty. Having come from an established middle-class background, he was destroyed by his loss of legal status and identity, the experience of joblessness, and the shame of living in poverty. He became consumed by rage, and our lives were ravaged by his violence.

Most of my early childhood in Telok Kurau, a Malay kampong along the east coast of Singapore, passed without incident. We lived as an intergenerational extended family—grandma with her children, my parents, my little brother and me. No one spoke of things that were painful or troubling, instead they tried to establish a sense of stability through a daily rhythm. This veneer of calm was disrupted one night when my father became violent. He stormed out of the house in a fit of rage, purposely crashed his boneshaker car into a coconut tree outside, and disappeared. We did not see him again for a long time—until he showed up one day when we least expected it. I was too young to understand what was happening, to know the terrible hopelessness that overwhelms people when they lose their source of livelihood.

After my father walked out on us, my mother became the main breadwinner of our household. As a child, I witnessed how hard she had to work to keep everyday life going. Our house in Telok Kurau was located far from her work place in Seletar. The office van would fetch her before six in the morning and she would only return after seven in the evening. As a woman, she could never earn enough to provide for all of us. Because of the long hours she spent working and travelling to and from work, she had little time to care for her children, her younger siblings, and her mother. Her marriage had already broken down but, as a Catholic, she was not allowed a divorce and she felt blamed for not being able to keep her family together. We were stigmatized as being a 'broken family'. My mother was trapped in this social landscape and had no space of her own to process what was happening. She fought with all her strength to change our living conditions but had reached her limits, stretched to a breaking point. There was no social support and little community empathy for a single mother with young children. I watched her weep in loneliness and despair a few days before she was hospitalized. A week later she died, aged twenty-six. She had lost the will to live.

* * *

I was six years old when my mother died. Making sense of life was not easy after her death. When they buried my mother, my cries drowned out everyone else's weeping. It was almost as if I sensed what was to come. The extended family was in so much grief that no one knew how to stop my father when he showed up a few days later to take my little brother and me to live with him and his new wife. We were suddenly torn away from grandma and the extended family. They were not allowed to visit us or to be in touch with us. There were no goodbyes—just shock and tears of disbelief.

During this next phase of our childhood, my little brother and I lived with our father and stepmother in a rented house in Prome Road. We tried to live a normal life. I remember some happy moments, but our family life was complicated and bewildering. On our first Christmas at Prome Road, my father bought a child's jeep for my little brother and a doll for me, whom I called Cinderella. This was his way of trying to bring some cheer to us, despite our precarious financial situation. It was during these years that my brother and I became more aware of our father's eccentricities—his volatile temperament and impulsive, at times misplaced, sense of adventure. I remember he once sent us out to the street to play in the monsoon, so that we could feel the tropical rain on our skin. On another occasion, my father took us for a day trip across the straits, to the waterfalls in Kota Tinggi in Johor. Just as my brother and I were savouring the splash of water on our backs, a group of men with guns appeared and ushered us out to safety. It was the first time I heard the words 'Communist Emergency'. My father had apparently brought us to forbidden territory. Not long afterwards, in 1956, my half-brother was born and I heard the words 'political riots' when an ambulance rushed my stepmother through the riots to the hospital for delivery. While helping to look after my baby stepbrother at home, I enjoyed drawing on the blackboard that was hanging in the living room, inspired by Buddha statues that my father had placed around the house. One day I drew the Laughing Buddha on the blackboard with colourful chalk. When my father saw it, he called my stepmother and exclaimed how beautiful it was. My stepmother's face fell and she insisted that I erase my drawing immediately. I never drew again. But, it did not stop me from observing the world around me.

Incidents such as these made me realize how vulnerable I was as a child to the idiosyncrasies of the adults at home. Perhaps it was then that a spirit of resistance began to stir imperceptibly within me. One Christmas, my father rented a car to bring us to visit his friends. On our way home, after several visits and many drinks, my father had difficulty keeping control of the wheel and the car skidded on to its side. Fortunately, no one was hurt. When we reached home, as I was getting out of the car from his side, my father banged the car door and my right thumb accidentally got caught in it. I managed to release my thumb but blood was flowing fast. My father pulled me into the house, prepared a purple liquid concoction and forced me to dip my thumb into it, followed by iodine. I screamed in pain but was told that I either did it or I would lose my thumb. I refused to let the adults hold my hand and thrust my thumb into the stinging solution. In my child language,

I cried out to them through my tears: 'Myself put!' On that day, I learned the need to take things into my own hands. If I had to endure pain, I would do it on my own terms.

I have no idea how my father earned his living, except that there was one room in the house where patients could come in for physiotherapy, homoeopathy, and other treatments. His patients were mostly middle-class individuals, some from Singapore, some from Indonesia. His home practice was not legally registered. One day, a female detective came undercover, pretending to seek treatment. She must have reported on him to the authorities—soon afterwards, he was forced to close down his informal practice and our family was stranded financially. Because my father was unable to sustain the household economically, we were all soon displaced and nearly became homeless. I spent the next six years in a community of migrants, in a slum area along the Singapore River where we were given free housing on the second floor of a shophouse on Teochew Street, next to a charcoal shop in front of Ellenborough Market.

Sinsehs, Storytellers, and Samsui Women

Our neighbourhood in Chinatown bustled with life. Lorries of fish and vegetables would come in by 3 a.m. every morning to be sorted for redistribution to other markets in Singapore. Old women would come by to pick the good parts of vegetables they could find in the waste left behind. Men sweating with bended backs carried heavy sacks of rice, gambier, and copra on their sinewy bodies, up and down the planks, from the tongkangs[3] that plied the Indonesian islands of Riau to the godowns along the river. The rats that jumped off the tongkangs were bigger and fiercer than the scrawny slum cats.

---

[3]   Tongkang means riverboat.

It was a bubbling kind of community with different dialect groups on every street; clanship and mutual-aid societies; Teochew storytellers and musicians; street operas during the month of the hungry ghosts; shrines, spirit mediums and temples; traditional sinseh[4] medicine shops; funeral parlours; triads; gambling dens; and opium smokers. This community was also a hotbed of radicalism, with various groups of competing ideological backgrounds struggling for greater rights and freedom. Many of these groups were workers, and some of them advocated self-determination and the overthrow of colonialism through political actions and workers' strikes. As all this unfolded on my doorstep, I encountered people's resilience in dealing with adverse social conditions—their creation of support systems and local networks, solidarity, and agency to change unjust social structures. I saw their political struggles; listened to their stories, dramas and debates; and witnessed the dignity with which they tried to live and work.

I was pushed into the world early, but the community became my canvas to observe. It was supposed to be a dangerous place, but, given the messiness of the place I called home, the streets had an energy and rhythm that I found fascinating as a child. I felt the pulse of the community, its strong sense of solidarity and dynamism. I was not afraid to venture out, as most people would greet me asking if I had eaten. It was a community that knew hunger and had escaped famine, and their survival tactics were evident in everything they did. I observed, for instance, that the workers who sorted the vegetables for redistribution, would not only remove the rotten parts but also leave some good parts for those who would rummage for scraps. Religion was deeply embedded in the community; it was a coherent social practice

---

[4]   A sinseh is a traditional Chinese doctor, often without proper certification.

that was integrated into everyday life to keep its balance and find a way to solve individual problems. There were shrines everywhere and gods for everything. Spirit mediums were at the centre of community life and commonly consulted. On the eighth month of every lunar year, rituals were carried out to appease the hungry ghosts with lavish layout of food, and Chinese opera of human drama were performed from noon to midnight to keep them entertained and satisfied while they wandered the human realm before returning to their abode. Networks built along clans collected funds from their businesses and provided local safety nets for those in need and relationship support for those who belonged in terms of dialect or surname.

In the sinseh shops, there was a cure for everything, prescribed by men who inherited traditional knowledge of Chinese medicine. Besides numerous herbs and roots of exotic plants, there were also rhino horns and dried seahorses, which I had a problem seeing as 'medicine'. Some mornings, along the street in front of the market, I saw turtles with their flippers pierced by wires that tied them to wheeled platforms. I felt their pain. I saw their tears and I cried with them. Later, I would find turtle soup, meat, and eggs being sold as nourishing food for workers in Chinatown. My mind would ask, 'Why? Was there no other way to keep the workers healthy?'

Although our mixed heritage family was somewhat excluded from the local support networks being organized in our largely Chinese community, my father was involved with a group of Malay pioneers of homoeopathic medicine. I remember frequent visits to our home in the latter half of the 1950s by 'Dr Burhanuddin' and his apprentices. This was, of course Dr Burhanuddin Helmi, the famed Malay nationalist, politician, and intellectual. Dr Burhanuddin, my father's colleague during their time in India, had written to Singapore's ministries of health and education to request for professional recognition of homoeopathic practitioners. Although his request was rejected, Dr Burhanuddin was granted permission to organize lectures, and he soon started informal lectures and study groups on homoeopathy at his house in Kampung Pachitan. My father contributed to these efforts to spread the knowledge of homoeopathic medicine in Malaya, including through training Dr Burhanuddin's apprentices at our house in Teochew Street. Still, the absence of professional recognition meant that my father could not practise his skills legally, and was not able to make a living and support the family.

During the six years that I lived in Chinatown with my father and stepmother, I experienced the desperation of poverty. Whatever little money we had was spent on alcohol for my father and romance comic books or visits to spirit mediums for my stepmother—'opium' to numb the pain of everyday hardship. As a result, my little brother and I were constantly hungry and often resorted to eating the leftover food from the gambling room downstairs. Despite the misery of daily life, my father tried, in vain, to cling to broken shards of joy and beauty—creating sculptures from plaster of Paris, or imitating Mario Lanza singing the 'Serenade' from the movie, *The Student Prince*. My father's 'rage against the dying of the light'[5] was ultimately futile, and I witnessed his gradual descent into despair. He vented his frustration and humiliation in violent outbursts and behaviour that tore apart any remaining semblance of a stable household.

Growing up in such an environment, I became outraged at how people were made vulnerable and insecure by forces that were, at times, beyond their control. It was the birth of my social consciousness and empathy. Without being aware that I was doing

---

[5] A famous line from Dylan Thomas's poem, 'Do not go gentle into that good night'.

so, I started questioning the social reality and the dysfunction I observed around me: How is it that people can work so hard, yet remain so poor? Why are they paid so little? Why are some people reduced to hopelessness and powerlessness without the possibilities of a different future? How can children be left so vulnerable? Most people in the community survived and some even thrived, but many also gave up on life and their bodies floated down the black waters of the Singapore River.

In the midst of all this, I saw that many women refused to accept discrimination in the existing social landscape and managed to change some of their living conditions through solidarity and redefining their own destinies. Some women in the community chose not to marry. Many were part of an anti-marriage movement of former silk workers from the Pearl River Delta in China. They had migrated as single women, resisted the feudal–patriarchal social order and marriages that devalued them, and established sisterhoods instead. As a child, I often noticed a group of these women squatting together at my street corner, eating their home-cooked lunch from tin mugs. They were the Samsui women, highly skilled construction workers, providing the hard labour that built the early houses and infrastructure of Singapore's city state. These women were easily identified by their red headwear and bright blue clothes, which they used almost as a statement of defiance.

There was also another group of women whom I watched when they walked down my street. They were the caregivers called the 'black-and-white amahs' because they put on starched, well-ironed white blouses with flowing black pants. The 'Black and Whites', as they were known, were not treated as 'live-in servants', although they were domestic workers. They were highly skilled in managing complex households and extended families, and it became a status symbol to employ them. These two groups of women used clothing as identity to indicate that they belonged to a specialized group of skilled women. Confronted by adverse conditions, they defined themselves by making their work so professional that they were highly valued and preferred by those who could afford to employ them. But, they and their sisterhoods, set their own rules and standards. Working conditions were collectively determined and discussed by the sisterhood—which functioned as a guild—before the amah took up a job. An abuse of one was regarded as an abuse of the whole, and met with the collective withdrawal of their services. These women were self-empowered. They created economic independence and identity based on solidarity and the dignity of their work.

My stepmother's brother-in-law had employed two 'black-and-white amahs' in his family mansion on 22 Cavenagh Road. These amahs supervised other domestic workers to manage the household and provide meals for the extended family and its vast and complex connections. Lavish spreads were prepared every day to feed four sittings at the large marble dining table. The first sitting was for the patriarchs—the grandfather, his wife and concubines, and his sons. The second sitting was for the sons' wives and their children. The third sitting was for poor relatives and those who had migrated from the Riau Islands as part of the family's trading networks. Finally, the fourth sitting was for the servants, chauffeurs, and their families.

My stepmother used to bring my little brother, my half-brother, and me for meals at this house on Cavenagh Road a few times a week, which brought some relief to our hunger. We were fed at the third sitting, along with other poor relatives. From the stories and conversations in this house, I learnt that the shophouse on Teochew Street where we lived, in fact, belonged to this family, and this was the reason why we were allowed to live there rent-free. I also learnt that my stepmother's family, whom we sometimes visited on Pulau Senggarang in the Riau Islands, was part of this trading network of gambier and copra that was controlled by the Cavenagh Road household. I was struck that the family was so generous in sharing the wealth generated from their business to provide social support for less privileged relatives as well as a community of workers in transit from Riau. At the same time, we all sensed the display of wealth and the hierarchy of power that was perpetuated through this benevolence. With every mouthful at the Cavenagh Road dining table, we were grateful to be fed, but made acutely aware of our dependency and our place in the social order of their universe.

Storms in Childhood

In the midst of the chaos of family life after my mother's death, I did not just lose my protector, I almost lost the gift of education, too. At the age of eight, I was not yet in school. When my grandmother found out about this, she went to see Father Bonamy, a Catholic priest from the Good Shepherd Cathedral, located not far from Chinatown. I have no idea how grandma and the extended family knew where we were staying, and about our precarious existence. All I remembered was that when my uncle located us in Prome Road and tried to see us, he was threatened and chased away. The priest, on the other hand, could not be so easily dismissed. Father Bonamy visited our household and was shocked by the vulnerability of our situation. But, he thought I was a bright, young girl, so I was immediately registered in an elite Catholic school. By that time I was overaged and had to catch up with students who had pre-school education.

The school opened up a new world for me, but it soon shifted its location from Kampong Java to Thomson Road. The new location was far from the house, and my experience of school changed. I had to wake up very early in the morning, walk carefully through the street to avoid the melting ice from the fish market staining my white school shoes, run quickly across Read Bridge to catch the first bus that was usually crowded and would often not stop, change buses, walk up a hill, and, yet, was still late for school. Despite my explanations, my name was added in the blacklist and I was detained regularly as a punishment for being late. I hardly had any books and found it extremely difficult to study, given the home environment. I never had the cleanest of uniforms and money for food or school fees, but survived through the generosity of my maternal aunt who secretly provided me with regular meals and pocket money. It was humiliating for me every month when the time came to pay the school fees. The nun in charge of the class, annoyed at the accumulation of late fees, would call me by my full name and make me stand up in front of the class to ask why a student with a European-sounding name like mine was unable to pay the fees. I began to dread the sound of my name being called out. Eventually, I could not speak my name without a stammer.

Being an elite school, it was detached from the social context of the Singapore River. It served a different segment of the society. The majority of students in the school were from the upper middle class, came in chauffeur-driven cars, had clean clothes, paid their fees on time, and were fully supported by their families to study and thrive. I quickly learned that we lived in the same country, but in different worlds—isolated and excluded from one another. There was a lack of empathy for other kinds of social experience, and rigidities and rules were imposed that did not accommodate children in vulnerable situations. In my most difficult moments at school, I experienced elitism, class arrogance, and social inequality. Grandma, who was not allowed to see me at home, came to the school on several occasions to wait for me at recess. She would be so excited on those days that she would wake up early to cook nourishing food, take the bus to the school, and wait for me. Several times, she couldn't wait any longer and wandered to my classroom to peep at me through the windows. To my horror, the teachers shooed her away as if she were a vagrant. Later, I was scolded and asked to tell my grandma that she was not allowed to come up to see me in the classroom. I tried to explain my complicated family situation to the teachers. Perhaps as a child I did not have the words to make them understand. I just felt broken as grandma never came to see me at school again.

Meanwhile, the place called home became a dangerous place for me. The social welfare system—an institution established to protect the vulnerable—could have helped, but it was nowhere to be seen in practice. When I eventually became a 'social welfare case', I was mortified to hear the senior official say that she wished my case did not come to her attention as it was complicated and would require too much of her time. My aunt brought gifts of fruits and biscuits to pacify her. When I was eventually placed in Mount Emily Girls' Home, I found myself locked up with girls who were classified as 'likely to escape'. My schooling was interrupted; we were taught sewing instead and put to the task of cleaning the Home and sorting the worm-infested vegetables for our meals. This defined my experience of 'charity'. Throughout my life, I have instinctively rejected charity and dependency, focusing instead on cultivating my own agency. I learned early that institutions and their leadership are imperfect, and cannot be trusted or relied to deliver genuine support when most needed.

During those dark days, I began trusting my intuition rather than the dysfunctional adults around me. I detached myself and retreated inwards, away from my hostile external environment. I created my own private oasis. In my silent world, the suffering inflicted by the external world and sublime grace somehow converged. I listened to my inner whisper and discovered my soul's strength to defy destiny and reimagine a different world. Although this was a period of scarcity and hardship for me, I felt an internal abundance. I found my ethical core, a force driven from within, and experienced the power of divine grace to transcend my fate, breaking the darkness with a prayer that I would be able to, one day, return to my grandmother's house. That prayer was eventually answered.

I was legally removed from my destructive father's home and sent to stay with my grandmother and my mother's siblings in Siglap, along the east coast of Singapore. It was a period of stability and opportunity for me. Yet, I could not shake off the deep pain of having to leave my little brother behind. After our mother's death, I had become his protector. I used to hold his hand wherever we went, guarding him against the unknown dangers of the outside world. Now I felt that I was leaving him alone to face the known dangers of the household, to the violence that was devouring our family.

A Time of Affirmation

My grandmother, Anna Ong Choo Lian, was the matriarch of the Siglap household. Despite having no formal education and only informal employment, she had managed to get out of poverty and give her children a better life. She had one clear goal in life—to build a stone house to protect her family. She achieved this through her instinctive resourcefulness and resolve. She had accumulated a small sum as part of a tontine system with other women. This sum, together with the earnings of her children and some savings that my mother had left behind, was enough to buy a piece of land along Siglap Road and construct a house on it. This became the family house, and remains so to this day. Although my mother's death had cast a long shadow on my grandmother's life, all her surviving children eventually did well for themselves—one aunt became secretary to the CEO of a British motor company, while another aunt became the first Asian Mother Provincial of the Convent of the Holy Infant Jesus throughout Malaysia. My uncle became one of the country's most sought-after maths tutors; he was deeply caring and invested in my education. Through him, I developed a joy of gardening, an appreciation of beauty, and the pleasure of reading. The extended family showered me with affection and I felt 'special'. The Siglap household was well-organized, stable with solid values. It had attained financial stability through discipline and hard work, and, later, even adopted two vulnerable children. It was a fortress that protected its inhabitants from the turbulence of the outside world.

Through all this, my grandmother never fully recovered from the grief of losing her eldest child, my mother. Often, when I was trying to study, my grandmother would seat herself outside the window of the room, and repeat the narrative of her life out loud—the hardships my mother and she had endured, the suffering and sorrow of the family upon the death of my mother, and the trauma of having her two grandchildren taken away. She believed that marriage was no escape from hardship, and that the only 'way out' for me as a young woman was through education and 'a strong brain'. Based on these convictions, she took great measures to develop and protect my brains—she used to feed me 'food for the brains' and soak my head in coconut oil so that my brains would not 'dry up' when I walked in the hot sun.

Perhaps it worked. It must have been through sheer determination that, despite the serious disruptions and pain, I did well enough in the primary school to remain in the A class, with the top students, throughout my years there. I was later transferred to Katong Convent for my secondary education. The atmosphere at Katong Convent was more relaxed and accepting of diversity. The school also saw something in me that I did not see in myself—leadership. I was made a prefect and trusted with overseeing our student community. We had a maths teacher, a nun whom we nicknamed 'Lobster' because her face often turned red and she seemed to always be in a rush. She would put us into groups, ask us to work out the maths problems among ourselves, and then quickly leave the class. Sometimes, we wondered if she knew any maths at all. Students who took private tuition were expected to lead the group. She would return towards the end of the class to ask for our answers. I was suddenly identified as one of the lead students. My uncle was an exceptional maths teacher, and I was trained by him. I sensed that I always had to be substantively strong to be of value to anyone.

St Andrew's Secondary School, where I did my pre-university education, further developed my leadership skills and celebrated when I won debates and the Chan Ah Kow Science Trophy at an inter-school competition. It was a time of affirmation. My mind was alive and absorbed the influences of novels written by female authors—*The Good Earth* by Pearl S. Buck, *Sold for Silver* by Janet Lim, *And the Rain My Drink* by Han Suyin. They all captured my imagination and resonated with the questions I was struggling with—how individual lives were affected by gender discrimination and the upheaval of the larger world. I was inspired to read about the life of Helen Keller, and her words resonated deeply with me: 'No pessimist ever discovered the secret of the stars, or sailed to an uncharted land or opened a new doorway to the human spirit.' My enjoyment of epic films also developed with *The Ten Commandments* and *Ben-Hur*. Supported by the nourishing environment of stability, I plunged myself into learning, graduated with a very strong Grade One and an equally strong Pre-University certificate from the British Cambridge education system of the time.

I gained admission to Singapore University, which eventually became the National University of Singapore. Attending university had been a distant dream while I was growing up in an impoverished and volatile household in Chinatown. This dream had now become a reality, and I was determined to make the most of this opportunity. As I was registering for courses, I decided to switch from natural sciences to social sciences. Deep down, I needed to make sense of society with its chaos and traumas. It was one of the best decisions I have ever made. The university, and the community it provided, nurtured the seeds of transformation within me—university education, and the several scholarships I was awarded, enlarged the contours of my life, gave me confidence, and positioned me for a future I never expected.

Since returning to my grandma's house, I was told that, legally, I was not allowed to be in touch with my little brother till he turned twenty-one. While I carried on with my new life, I waited impatiently for his twenty-first birthday. On that day, I woke up early, rushed to the phone directory, and turned the pages till the name and number of the shophouse on Teochew Street. I kept repeating a silent prayer for divine intervention till it was a decent time to make the phone call. The phone was picked up by someone on the ground floor who shouted for my brother. He finally came, and I heard his voice well after a decade. We reconnected instantly and decided to meet in person rather than speak on the phone.

When we finally met, we just hugged each other and decided not to ask questions that had no answers, not to dwell on matters better left unspoken. We were just happy to be in each other's company and know that we survived with grace. There was not a trace of bitterness in either of us, we just felt regret about our stolen childhood together. As our eyes met, I accepted that this was how life wanted to reveal its wounds and its mysteries to us. As we spoke, my brother finally told me that they were to become homeless again, as the shophouse was to be demolished by the government as the first wave of the urban renewal scheme. The street and all it stood for—unkempt, uncontrollable—was not a reality to be emulated in modern Singapore. They were offered a small three-room public Housing & Development Board (HDB), flat but had no resources to put the down payment. I informed my aunt that I was in contact once more with my brother and of their predicament. She immediately took action and said that she kept his share of the savings my mother left and would release it to him to buy the flat, knowing fully well that it will also be housing those who caused so much sorrow to the family.

While we each carry unspoken histories, I live in wonder at how my little brother grew up to be one of the kindest souls I know. While he did not have the opportunity for university education, the moment he started earning from work, he sent our half-brother for higher education. My brother eventually rose through the ranks and studied at night to get the necessary education to become the industrial relations manager of a huge multinational company operating in Singapore. I eventually met my half-brother in secret. He was brilliant and talented—a black belt holder in karate and an artist, he eventually became the regional director of a major multinational pharmaceutical company. My brother was his anchor in his growing-up years, and together they brought the family out of poverty.

During these years of childhood and young adulthood, I experienced how the texture of our private and public lives is shaped by events and institutions larger than ourselves. Hidden in the dark shadows of our vast historical canvas are the more intense dramas of real families and communities, impacted by political

forces, social arrangements, and attitudes of the time. These are
the realities of women, men and children, the unfolding of their
personal tragedies and courage, as they live through rampant
discrimination, violence, and suffering. Even when communities
and extended families tried to provide protection during upheavals,
they were often stretched beyond their capacity. Established
institutions that could have helped people at the margins often
failed miserably to understand and, therefore, to provide safety
nets and social protection when these were most needed.

Out of this social landscape emerges another drama—people
who refused to be locked into their social conditions and history,
those who had the consciousness to know that institutions are
imperfect and that systems fail but can be reformed through
better leadership, those who had the moral imagination and
courage to change the social arrangements that created abuse and
discrimination. I saw that the human spirit finds ways to transform
the trajectory of vulnerability. I was determined to transform my
life, urged by my belief in the power of people to shape their
own lives and define their own destinies. I dared to dream and
envision a different world where people have the power to initiate
change and cocreate history, each struggle bringing us closer to
the possibility of a greater humanity.

2

Aspirations and Frustrations

'Unless we aim for the seemingly unattainable, we risk settling for mediocrity.'

—*Sergio Vieira de Mello*

Emerging from the unspeakable horrors and suffering of the Second World War, the world was reimagining a different future, finding pathways to transform and rebuild anew. The global search for freedom, peace, and shared prosperity ignited unprecedented international solidarity and social movements worldwide. I discovered this world with its social aspirations and political drama as I embarked on my further education. It awakened and unfolded in fragments through many conversations, the relationships I built, and the characters and circumstances I encountered during this period of my life.

I entered university when decolonization and the formation of new nations were in full swing. It was an era characterized by new hopes and fears as colonial power structures disintegrated, replaced by aspirations for freedom by new nations that were determined to control their own destinies. These were frustrated by heightened world tensions due to the Cold War rivalry between what emerged as the capitalist and communist blocs, competing to shape the new international order. Outside our formal lectures, my fellow students and I engaged in debates and discussions about the implications of different pathways to nation-building and political principles for newly independent states. It was our political awakening. We asked ourselves: What was the right path for Singapore—democracy, socialism, capitalism, or a creative combination of all? What were the benefits and consequences of each path? And, which path would bring the greatest good to the largest number of people? These questions were not theoretical; they were real choices. They were of immediate importance, given the new geopolitical reality of the Cold War that Singapore and other newly independent countries found themselves in.

It was in this context that I joined the Democratic Socialist Club (DSC)—a student association at Singapore University that focused on understanding the political and economic trends affecting Singapore and the region. Initiated by two medical students—Loo Choon Yong and Alfred Loh—the DSC organized regular readings and discussions to educate its members about political and social change as well as events with political leaders, including then Prime Minister Lee Kuan Yew. Choon Yong was the main force behind DSC, recruiting members and inspiring new members through ideas and intense discussions. He was determined to have some young women in leadership positions; he encouraged me to read and speak up, and gave me confidence that I could be the DSC's international secretary and appointed me when I was ready.

Within this small group of committed university students, we read profusely, engaged in intense discussions, theorized and reflected on the political drama around us, and attempted to understand and explain the political changes impacting our lives. A key question that kept coming up in our debates was how our region came to be at the centre of the Cold War. Many newly independent nations, including Singapore, were caught between the mutually exclusive approaches and binary opposition of the two superpowers engaged in the Cold War. In Singapore, this global clash of ideologies had affected political life and choices at the national level in many ways, including the arrest and detention without trial of political leaders regarded as sympathetic to the communist bloc. Strict restrictions were suddenly placed on labour organizing—the mode of mobilization and struggle for political independence—and on students' political discussions in universities, especially in Chinese educational colleges, which were considered to be fertile soil for the sowing of communist ideas. As socially engaged students, the turbulence of the times made us somewhat nervous. However, it conferred a sense of urgency in the questions we were asking and forced us to think through multiple implications of our strategies and actions with seriousness and caution, as new nations became caught in the intersection of superpower interests.

We witnessed the Cold War rivalry worsening with the rise of China, the gains in territories and population under communism, and the fear of the 'domino effect' in Asia. Superpower politics made the future of the 'underdeveloped countries' a major part of their foreign policy, as the process of decolonization gained momentum in the 1950s and early 1960s. The political allegiance or neutrality of emerging nations became an important stake in the big struggle for world power and security. New nations were kept in the respective spheres of influence of the contending power blocs not only through large-scale support to economic development and state-building, but also through brutal conflicts and wars along ideological lines. Despite the Bandung Non-Aligned Movement's attempts to avoid ideological confrontation, our own neighbourhood—South East Asia—became the primary global geopolitical hotspot. The region was set on fire by both sides of the Cold War—there was the raging Vietnam War, the mass killings in

Indonesia of those accused of being communist sympathizers, the killing fields and genocide by the Khmer Rouge in Cambodia, the less visible war with its cluster bombs in Laos, and the massacre in East Timor. Millions of innocent civilians paid with their lives, or became refugees to escape the nightmare and cannibalism of war. In another part of Asia, when the Soviets invaded Afghanistan, the US aided and armed the local mujahideen, creating a 'green belt' of Islamic fighters to defeat Soviet communism. It was a time of great divides and disruption.

These global ideological divisions were played out in our own intellectual circles. Like other politically engaged student groups, the activities of the DSC came under the scrutiny of the authorities. The DSC was seen as more moderate than the Socialist Club that was also active in the university, although the president of the DSC, Choon Yong, regularly attended the International Socialist Youth meetings. We were well-connected internationally with European, New Zealand, and British Labour parties and student leaders. Together with friends like Helen Clark[6], Mike Moore[7] and others, we felt that we were part of history in the making and that we could help chart its course by engaging and becoming active in our respective contexts. Many countries coming out of colonialism regarded themselves as democratic socialist, and the DSC was part of the global movement of youth leaders from these countries. The DSC was regularly invited to international conferences and exposure programmes.

---

[6]   Helen Clark became the first woman to be elected Prime Minister of New Zealand and served for three successive terms (1999–2008). She was also the first female Administrator of the United Nations Development Programme (2009–17).

[7]   Mike Moore became the Prime Minister of New Zealand (1990) and the Director-General of the World Trade Organization (1999–2002).

Within my first year at university, at the age of twenty, I was chosen by Choon Yong, in my capacity as international secretary of the DSC, to go on a three-month visit to Europe and the Scandinavian countries to study what was termed the 'Middle Way' or the 'Third Way'. It was an eye-opening experience, and significantly shaped the way I understood the unfolding of the external world. The group I travelled with consisted of a union leader from Mumbai (India), an elderly Argentinian couple who were members of the Peronist political movement, and an Israeli leader from a kibbutz—a collective farm settlement. I was the youngest in the group, the most inexperienced with neither political nor organizing background. They all must have wondered why I was even there. However, thrown into the midst of their company, I imbibed as much as I could from their background and experience. Travelling overland by van for weeks on end, we became close companions with bonds forged through discussions on the road and personal stories at meal times. We opened up fascinating worlds to each other and became part of each other's intellectual drama.

Many of my companions were part of the political and historical landscape of their countries and regions. Through their narratives, I sensed a complex interplay of personal idealism with chaotic political forces. There was the drama of contradictions between working-class sympathies and authoritarianism in Peronist Argentina, as it struggled for social justice, economic independence, and political sovereignty. I learnt of the close interaction between unions and political parties in India that transformed the 'jewel in the crown' of the British Empire into the world's largest democracy, yet kept its caste structure intact. In Israel, there was the aftermath of the Holocaust and the sheer determination of Israelis to establish and fight for their own state, yet the inability to achieve the two-state solution and resolve the Israeli–Palestinian conflict.

Our overland trip started from Vienna in Austria, then my companions and I travelled to major towns in Germany, Belgium, Denmark, Norway, Finland, Sweden, France, and ended in Salzburg (Austria). In each place, we were hosted by the leaders of the Socialist International or the democratic socialist movement, most of whom were in the government. We visited many cooperatives, and had discussions with leaders from the labour movements, ministers, parliamentarians, mayors, and university students. We visited families and were treated to numerous community and cultural events. We had the privilege of listening to Olof Palme from the Social Democratic Party, who later became the Prime Minister of Sweden for two terms. He spoke with pride about being a social democrat and delivering the promise of social security through solidarity with fiscal sustainability. He warned us of the brutality of communism, with its dictatorship and violence as experienced during the years of Stalin's Great Purge. He impressed on us the need to forge the 'Third Way' to balance collective responsibility with individual freedoms and control capitalist greed for power and privilege that can also destroy us. Years later, he was assassinated. We also engaged with Ivan Illich, a Croatian–Austrian philosopher and Catholic priest, on his book *Deschooling Society* published in 1971. He spoke to us about reinventing learning to inspire minds through 'educational webs' facilitated by technology so that each of us can have the opportunity for lifelong learning and sharing.

In Stockholm, I had the privilege to have lunch and a long walk with Professor Gunnar Myrdal, the 1974 Nobel Laureate of Economics. He had undertaken 'an inquiry into the poverty of nations', focusing on Asia and capturing its drama of poverty and 'underdevelopment' in his three volumes entitled *The Asian Drama*. He gave me the books, a gift to remind me of our long conversation about creating a new development trajectory by changing entrenched power relationships, social attitudes, and institutional structures. His message was clear—our future lies in our own hands and it need not be tragic. I was fascinated by these intense interactions and experiences. They awakened and focused my interest to seriously study the social and political issues of our time and pursue the greater ideals that were remaking our external realities so that human life could be less painful, kinder, and more hopeful.

At an international conference in Salzburg, one of the Asian leaders I met was Fan Yew Teng, the acting secretary general of the Democratic Action Party (DAP) of Malaysia. The conference participants were attending a concert featuring the music of Salzburg's most famous son, Wolfgang Amadeus Mozart. Just before the first notes of Mozart's *Clarinet Concerto* rose from the orchestra, I saw Fan Yew Teng walk into the concert hall. He was magnetic and I was immediately drawn to him. He was handsome and stylish in a classic, worldly sense—he exuded charisma, confidence, and an aura of powerful energy. The lights dimmed and the music began, and my impression of Fan Yew Teng accompanied me throughout the concert.

While many of us at university were engaged in discussions and debates, Fan Yew Teng, at the age of twenty-six, was already directly involved in political activism and representation of communities through his position as a parliamentarian. He was the youngest and most vocal Member of Parliament[8]. By the time I met him, he had already, as an educator and union leader, co-organized a nationwide teachers' strike in 1967 and successfully achieved equal pay for women in the teaching profession, as well as housing, medical, and pension benefits for all teachers in

---

[8]   Fan Yew Teng was Member of Parliament for Kampar (elected in 1969) and Menglembu (elected in 1974).

Malaysia. For this, he had been exiled to teach in remote areas by the then minister of education. With his irrepressible spirit, he not only survived but also thrived in these areas, cultivating a sense of solidarity with ordinary people and enjoying the relaxed rhythm of the rural environment while still being concerned about the future of his country and its people.

On the second day of the conference in Salzburg, to my surprise, I found Yew Teng sitting beside me. He had swapped places with Vassant, the labour unionist from India. Vassant later confessed to me that Yew Teng had persuaded him to exchange places, saying, 'You've spent enough time with her, please let me sit next to her.' Yew Teng and I engaged in hours of meaningful conversation, and went for walks in the Mirabell Gardens and springtime mountains of Salzburg. He was not only charismatic and handsome, but was also a caring person with a vibrant and generous spirit. We fell deeply in love. It was a meeting of souls as much as a meeting of hearts. By the end of our time in Salzburg, we were inseparable.

Soon after we returned to South East Asia, Yew Teng started visiting me regularly in Singapore. We used to go for long walks in the Botanical Gardens and along the seaside, immersed in endless conversations about life. Yew Teng became my emotional anchor. The gateway of my heart opened for the first time and love flooded in like an ocean. I experienced a side of Yew Teng that no one else knew. He was a true romantic at heart. He would write poetry to me, send me roses, and compare our love to that of Doctor Zhivago and Lara of Boris Pasternak's classic novel, a love that endures the upheavals of history. His first gift to me was a photograph of himself, on which he wrote these words: 'You are spring to me. All things to me. You are life itself'. He signed off every message to me with 'All My Love Always', and the acronym AMLA was engraved into our wedding rings when we eventually married. Yew Teng's belief in love was powerful, just like his belief in his ideals. Over the years, I watched him turn his social ideals into reality—closing the gap between idealism and personal commitment, dedicated to raising the quality of life of those around him. This often came at great personal cost.

At the Edge of a Volcano

After a few intense months of being immersed in socio-political discussions across Europe, I returned to the reality back home. I was fully charged, determined to strengthen my understanding of our social context and the critical issues facing it, to put away the sadness of my childhood, to concentrate on the hard work of transforming myself through education and societal engagement. The University of Singapore, with lecturers recruited from top universities of the world, created a vibrant learning environment, introducing us to reading materials, theoretical frameworks, and different perspectives on issues from around the globe. It provided me with my first serious exposure to intellectual analysis and instilled in me respect and tolerance for differences in academic discourse.

My professors in sociology, anthropology, political science, and philosophy, in particular, fostered my courage to inquire and be an independent learner. Many placed emphasis on fieldwork in local communities, social observation, data collection, and empirical research on real-life problems. I was emotionally connected to social analysis and tried to make what we studied relevant to my own experiences of the communities I observed in my childhood and adolescence. There is no better way of learning than being actively and critically engaged, but I had to struggle very hard to reclaim my voice, overcome my fears, and develop my communication skills. I wanted to express myself in words, but my thoughts were confusing and my feelings buried far too deep. I feared that I may touch wounds that were still raw. While I was emotionally connected to social analysis to clarify and help me disentangle jumbled thoughts, there was nothing yet to share as I was still a long way from understanding the workings of the social world and its interplay with individual lives. Science and mathematics were so much easier for me to articulate as a student, as they had clear rules that could be articulated. But since I chose social science as my prism of understanding, failure was not an option for me. I was determined to find a way of communicating that could be better heard and understood. My deeply caring uncle invested in my voice and drama training, as he witnessed me stammer as I tried to utter certain words associated with painful past experiences. It was a slow process, but eventually my exploration brought me back to the internal space and the inner whispers that guided me through the dark days of childhood. It was here that my voice, communication skills, and courage developed.

Despite these difficulties, I topped the sociology class of 1971, and Singapore University subsequently awarded me a research scholarship for my master's degree. A year later, I received another scholarship from the Ford Foundation to pursue my PhD at Cambridge University. Throughout my university journey, I focused on making sense of social-political history and how it interacts with people's lives and choices. In Cambridge, I spent hours in the library going through the archives on the struggle for political independence and literature on building the 'developmental state' to overturn historical vulnerabilities. Some of the reading material provided me with historical insights and perspectives into realities I had witnessed growing up by the Singapore River.

I began to understand the workings of imperialism and colonialism, as well as peoples' resistance against these power structures in order to define their own destinies. A major aspiration of newly independent nations was to shape the collective future by nurturing national leaders, building strong public institutions, delivering social security, and transforming peoples' consciousness from subject to citizen. I was inspired by how anti-colonial nationalist leaders such as Jawaharlal Nehru, Jomo Kenyatta, and Julius Nyerere strove for a new social contract between people and the nation, founded on trust, a shared vision of freedom and justice, and wise stewardship that would uplift the daily lives of ordinary people. However, the actual process of nation-building was much more chaotic and frustrating than anticipated. Undoing the legacy of colonialism meant decolonizing not only territorial, political, and economic relations, but also the minds of the people. The writings of Frantz Fanon on the mind of the colonizer and the colonized, in his book, *The Wretched of the Earth*, particularly interested me. As a psychiatrist and political philosopher, Fanon was concerned with the psychopathology of colonization and the human, social, and cultural aspects of decolonization. I was interested in his ideas of alienation, double consciousness, and racism.

Besides the immense challenges of decolonization and nation-building, new geopolitical blocs and alliances were at work, reconfiguring the world map along ideological fault lines. The choices made by political leaders of newly independent nations were influenced by the politics of the Cold War and the confines of the policy spaces it allowed. From the shaping of national identity, citizenship, and rights, the planning for development, to the nature of governance and citizens' engagement, there were political limits and unseen consequences determined by the Cold War divide that was now casting its long shadow on our societies, still reeling from the legacy of our colonial history.

While still studying, I was unprepared for the pending political storms surrounding me, which would eventually have an impact on my choices and life's direction. Identity politics and ethnonationalism were rife in the region. Despite the fact that South East Asia comprises greatly diverse cultures, identities, belief systems, and affiliations, leaders of the new nation states placed emphasis on politically constructed religious and ethnic identities forged during the colonial period and perpetuated by the Cold War. Nuanced aspects of pluralism, including within a religious or ethnic group, were downplayed at precisely the wrong moment. All this was played out in Singapore and Malaysia as they entered nationhood—together for a brief period during the formation of Malaysia in 1963, and then separately after they parted ways in 1965. The formation of Malaysia involved the difficult interplay of power relationships, and the defining and redefining of national identity and citizenship rights. In the process, politically constructed racial–religious identities were imposed on a complex society made up of indigenous, native, and immigrant communities. This often led to serious social and political tensions, and eventually resulted in Singapore's eviction from Malaysia.

The only Peoples' Action Party (PAP) candidate of Singapore to have won a parliamentary seat in the 1964 Malaysian general election was Devan Nair[9], a trade unionist and an anticolonial leader. He established the Democratic Action Party (DAP) before returning to Singapore after serving his term in the Malaysian Parliament. Chen Man Hin, Lim Kit Siang and Fan Yew Teng were recruited as key leaders of the new party. By the time I first

---

[9]   Devan Nair was the first Secretary-General of the National Trades Union Congress of Singapore, which he founded. He later served as President of Singapore from 1981 to 1985.

met Yew Teng, Malaysia had experienced its worst racial riots on 13 May 1969. Kit Siang, the secretary general of the party was detained without trial and Yew Teng himself, as acting secretary general, was in danger. He was the mobilizing and intellectual force that inspired and kept the party together while Kit Siang was in prison. At our first meeting in a coffee shop after his release, Kit Siang, on learning that I had become close to Yew Teng, said to me, 'You are standing at the edge of a volcano.' I had no idea what he meant till much later. Our lives unfolded against the rapid torrent of history. Politics was never far away, and it left its mark on all our personal relationships.

Devan Nair, who was then the head of the National Trades Union Congress, became a very dear friend and mentor to Yew Teng and me. We spent many evenings at his home in discussions about everything from world literature to Indian music, from his own struggle in prison as a freedom fighter for Singapore's independence to the philosophy of Sri Aurobindo and the purpose of politics. I was particularly close to Dhanam, Devan's wife, who treated me as a goddaughter, shared her own political stories, and would cook the most delicious meals for us.

It was Devan who called me the morning I was leaving to take the first paper of the final examination for my bachelor's degree in 1971. Yew Teng had been arrested for sedition. As editor of his party's newspaper, he had published an article promoting multiracialism and equal citizenship to break away from the colonial identity politics of 'divide and rule'. These were regarded as tabooed issues at that time, as they were seen as challenging the special rights of the Malays. This was not Yew Teng's intention as much as the need to pay attention to vulnerable citizens irrespective of ethnicity and to warn against nation-building that created winners and losers based on identity, rather than building a social foundation for all. I was deeply shaken by the arrest, but decided to complete my exams before leaving to see him, several days later. Yew Teng was eventually convicted, thrown out of parliament to silence his voice, and lost all his pension rights. But nothing could destroy the rebel in him or his spirit—joyful, generous, and simple to the end.

Paths to Nationhood

Yew Teng's arrest took place at a time when the new nation states of South East Asia were shaping their development trajectories while defining their alliances and position in the emerging world order. After being expelled from Malaysia in 1965, Singapore regarded that its only chance for survival as a small island surrounded by larger neighbours and an uncertain political climate was to be pragmatic and quickly transform itself from a colonial entrepôt into a modern city state. To do this, the country embraced a liberal economic system focused on forging economic integration with the changing global marketplace.

The process of nation-building in Singapore was not simple or linear. The journey of forging a sense of collective purpose and creating institutions to manage a common future was fraught with difficulties. There were very intense political and ideological struggles over the appropriate path to nationhood and development, leading to the mass arrest of political and union leaders. In 1964, Singapore saw a series of racial riots on issues of special rights, religion, and privileges. Between 1963 and 1966, the country found itself at the forefront of Konfrontasi—the low-intensity conflict sparked by Indonesia's opposition to the formation of the Federation of Malaysia seen as 'neocolonialism', during which Singapore experienced a series of bombings by Indonesian saboteurs. Indeed, the years following independence were a jagged period made even more difficult by the Cold War, sectarian violence, and tensions in the region.

After independence, Singapore quickly decided on the path to economic and social development. Under the vision and leadership of founding Prime Minister, Lee Kuan Yew, the Singapore government invested in healthcare, public housing, education, and infrastructure, and established a system based on multiracialism and meritocracy. This was the Singapore that I benefited from, a nation that emphasized quality education irrespective of race, religion, class, and gender.

As the country struggled against colonialism and prepared for political independence, women who were interested in social reforms worked tirelessly to ensure that the issues affecting women were on the political agenda, and that they were an integral part of nation-building. Female activists in Singapore formed the Singapore Council of Women (SCW), to provide a united voice for women, start a movement against polygamy and child marriage, and campaign for women's legal rights. The tenacity of these women paid off when the Peoples' Action Party (PAP) of Singapore included women's legal rights in the party's election manifesto in the 1959 election and passed the Women's Charter in 1961. It was a period of social change and a victory for women.

The 1964 riots were communal racial disturbances between the Malays and Chinese in Singapore following its merger with Malaysia. As I read about these riots, I finally understood the incident around the birth of my half-brother in 1956. Those riots broke out in the Chinese community when Chinese schools were closed and the Chinese Middle School Union was dissolved by the chief minister of Singapore with the support of the British governor. Chinese schools were accused of being communist, influenced by China. Later, I learned that Devan Nair was one of the union leaders arrested during this riot and only released when the PAP came to power in 1959, and Singapore began self-rule. I was shocked to discover that during that time even the Singapore Women's Association was banned as being 'pro-communist' as they mobilized against polygamy and child marriage, and campaigned for women's legal rights. These were all issues that affected my grandma and mother's generation and female pioneers in Singapore wanted to make sure that my generation did not inherit these social ills.

Economic transformation in the region brought its own drama. To create prosperity, generate jobs, and climb out of poverty, new nations had to address the economic devastation of World War II. There were also challenges and opportunities facing countries that had been integrated differently into the international economy during the age of empire, and now stood at very different stages of development. Some parts of Asia, such as Indonesia and Malaysia, were integrated as plantation economies or primary commodity exporters; others as manufacturers; and others still, including Singapore, as trading hubs, navy bases, and entrepôts.

The pathways to nationhood shaped by Singapore's leaders provided the ladders of social mobility for many, including my family. I benefited from quality education independent of gender and ethnicity. My brother and half-brother benefited from quality investment in public housing, and especially from the employment in foreign multinational corporations investing in the country and the recruitment of Singaporeans into their upper echelons. However, many found themselves in the lower echelon of the labour-intensive manufacturing industries located in the export processing zones (EPZs) that depended on non-unionized cheap labour. As Singaporeans moved out of this sector, low-waged migrants flowed in from neighbouring countries.

Singapore pursued rapid growth and technological catch-up based on attracting foreign investment, including those that maximized profits through low-cost migrant labour. It established its first export processing zones in the late 1960s and early 1970s, inviting labour-intensive export manufacturing industries for global markets to the Jurong industrial site. This early development of labour-intensive multinational supply chain was so successful that full employment was reached by 1972 and there was shortage of labour. The import of migrant workers became an economic strategy and prolonged employers' dependence on low-cost labour to maintain competitiveness for manufacturing, shipyards, as well as construction, given the rapid urban renewal and infrastructure development of the city state. Hence, the economic transformation of Singapore attracted young male and female migrant workers from the neighbouring countries, especially Chinese Malaysians who were migrating for economic and political reasons.

Labour, Life, and Leadership

It was Yew Teng who first got me interested in understanding the lives and challenges of female migrant workers in Singapore. Whenever Yew Teng visited me in the early 1970s, he never failed to visit the Malaysian migrant workers in the Jurong Industrial Estate. Many came from the 'new villages' that had been created by the Briggs Plan of the British to segregate and resettle about 500,000 Chinese villagers during the Malayan anti-communist emergency. Many were from his constituency, and he regularly took them out for dinner, listening to their plight. Most of them worked at construction sites and shipyards, where some workers lost their lives because of poor working conditions and shipyard fires. Yew Teng used to bring these concerns and cases to the attention of Devan Nair. As I listened to the discussions, I became increasingly interested in the labour movement of Singapore, the issues it could take on, and the changes it was going through.

I was particularly concerned about the situation of young migrant female workers, who were fuelling our prosperity through cheap labour, accepting low-quality manufacturing jobs during the early phase of our industrialization, but had no rights and representation.

The Catholic Church also had a strong influence on my intellectual development. While at secondary school and university, I was exposed to some of the best thinkers of the church. These were the people who were instrumental in shaping my mental strength, power of analysis, and, later on, the nature of my leadership. The head of the Jesuit order for Asia, Father Liam Egan—an exceptional Irish priest—was in charge of the Catholic students at the University of Singapore and became my spiritual mentor and a very close friend, guiding me in many aspects of my life. There was also Father Arro, the French chaplain of the Young Christian Students (YCS), who, with his white beard and sparkling eyes, introduced us to the idea that leadership was about 'doing ordinary things extraordinarily well'. The YCS encouraged us to read and reflect before we act. I was introduced to Teilhard de Chardin's writings—*The Future of Man* and *The Phenomenon of Man*—and his understanding of the convergence of faith in the cosmic divine and faith in our world—the 'two springs of energy' that have the potential to move us forward. These Irish and French priests, as well as the Franciscan nuns who were involved with student leadership training, all played a major role in directing my energy and compassion towards a more universal 'human community' beyond the boundaries of ideology, ethnicity, class, and religion. They gave me a new way of thinking about the world based on a much higher principle of social justice, a sense of moral commitment and courage, an understanding that development must have an ethical base to benefit all people.

In the 1970s, the church provided support to the young migrant workers at a time when no other social services existed for them. I decided to help. To understand first-hand the oppressive living and working conditions that the young migrant women described and the support they needed, I took up a job in a textile factory in Jurong for six months, staying in the workers' dormitory. The working hours were long, with most factory girls working double shifts as salaries were low. Their work was seen as temporary, which allowed for insecure contracts and the suppression of collective bargaining. The young women were heavily dependent on their male supervisors to keep their jobs, and even to be allowed toilet breaks. There were severe health and safety hazards, with loud machine noise and dust and cotton flying everywhere. Despite the difficult conditions, there were spaces for collective interaction and female solidarity in the dormitories where the young women could exchange their experiences, share meals, and reflect on how to deal with their problems on the factory floor. Unfortunately, in those days, an active citizenry, even if simply to understand and improve the lives of migrant workers, was not appreciated by the State and multinational companies. In our idealism, many of us had hoped that Singapore could lead an economic transformation that would not be rooted in cheap migrant labour, that it could break away this colonial model to recognize the dignity and rights of all workers as new nations developed their directions for progress. Many people paid the price for involvement when the government took punitive action against them, including political detention.

With my scholarship, Yew Teng and I decided to start a new chapter of our life in Cambridge, and, a few years later, in Princeton University, where Yew Teng was awarded the Parvin Fellowship at the Woodrow Wilson School of Public and International Affairs. It was in both these intellectual environments that we were exposed to the writings of Frankfurt School sociologists Herbert Marcuse and Jürgen Habermas and the so-called 'dependency theory' thinkers like Andre Gunder Frank and F.H. Cardoso, who later became the President of Brazil. These scholars tried to provide the analytical frameworks to help us understand what was happening to Third World economies and societies in transition, as well as the boundaries that limit inclusive growth and the potential for the global economy to be more humane.

In Cambridge, I was part of a discussion group initiated by fellow student Martin Khor—who was to become a lifelong friend and colleague—to debate different economic frameworks and theories and their implications for economic justice and the working class. These discussions continued when we returned to Singapore to do our fieldwork. Here, our discussion groups widened to include people like Ho Kwon Ping, newly returned from Stanford University, where he had been active in the anti-Vietnam War movement, and starting as a journalist at the *Far Eastern Economic Review*. Some of us shared a house in Barbary Walk, which became a kind of salon for engaged intellectuals; idealistic students; and young, socially committed professionals. I took over the room from my friend Tan Lian Choo, in the house rented by our colleague Peggy Tan. Our regular visitors included Ang Swee Chye and Ho Kwon Ping's sister, Ho Minfong. Unfortunately, this special place that forged many enduring friendships and nourished many young minds was raided and shut down just a few days after I returned to Cambridge, and some of our housemates were detained.

It was clear that our society was not yet ready for the exploration of different views or the role of critical thinking as a force for positive economic and social change. Our small island state was struggling with the politics of survival and saw 'no alternative' to its chosen path. Influenced by the ideological mindset and politics of the Cold War, the response to our intellectual inquiry and debates was a fear that in the process of exploring we could develop 'Marxist tendencies' which, if allowed to take root, could become 'threats to stability and national security'. It was only with the collapse of the Berlin Wall in 1989, the dissolution of the Soviet Union in 1991, and the opening up of China by 1992, that our world became less polarized and our societies more accommodating to civil discourse and engagement on the larger development agenda without ideological labelling. By then, my intellectual awakening had already evolved into a deeper quest for freedom, particularly the rights of women to be the decision-makers, shaping their future; contributing their insights; and deciding on the kind of households we want to live in, the societies we want to help build, and the types of institutions we want to work for. I was determined to find my own voice and direction, inspired by the mentors who helped me make sense of the harsh realities I saw around me and urged on by the desire to contribute to social transformation for greater fairness and dignity.

3

Navigating the Labyrinth

'Hope cannot be said to exist, nor can it be said not to exist. It is just like roads across the earth. For actually the earth had no roads to begin with, but when many pass one way, a road is made.'

—*Lu Xun*

The next phase of my life taught me the joys and responsibilities of marriage, motherhood, and a professional career. It was an exciting period, as I began to understand the possibilities and consequences of my life choices. I felt empowered by my education and life experience. However, navigating the labyrinth of institutions and social situations was a journey that revealed to me the best and worst of human nature, and made me define and assert my own ideas, ethics, and values.

After our marriage, I returned to Cambridge in 1975 to complete my PhD in Sociology. Yew Teng decided to put politics on hold to join me in Cambridge. However, he did not join me immediately. Although we had a special relationship and deep love for each other, Yew Teng was a private person and seldom shared his own worries, what he was struggling with, and the actions he would be taking. These often came as surprises to me. I had no idea that he had developed a fear of flying and could not join me in Cambridge as I had expected. He just said, 'Be patient and I will come.' I was used to our long-distance relationship since we first met, but this was most unexpected. In late 1975, he took a ship from Port Klang in Malaysia to Madras in India, and travelled by train up to New Delhi. There, Yew Teng came across a British tour bus that was about to depart for Istanbul and make its way onwards to the United Kingdom. He decided to take this overland journey from India, through Pakistan, Afghanistan, Iran, Turkey, Greece, and Europe to eventually join me in England. This overland journey in the depths of winter took over three months. After a long period of separation and receiving his postcards from various locations, I was glad to have him by my side again.

The years 1977 and 1978 were life-changing for us. I was completing my PhD in Sociology at Cambridge, while Yew Teng was at Princeton University pursuing his Parvin Fellowship. Since Yew Teng preferred not to fly, we travelled across the Atlantic together on the Polish ship, the TSS Stefan Batory. We could only afford to travel on the lower deck, and Yew Teng was constantly seasick from the rough waves. When we arrived back in Cambridge, I suddenly became ill, and thought perhaps it was a delayed reaction of a virus I contracted at sea. However, when I went for a medical check-up, I was told that I was pregnant with twins. My elation at this news was accompanied with some anxiety because we were living off our scholarships and struggling to make ends meet. Yew Teng was overjoyed by the news of my pregnancy; if he was at all worried he did not show it. One thing in particular was of grave concern to both of us—I had recently been exposed to German measles through our landlord's child. It was known to cause deformities in babies and the doctors recommended abortion, if necessary. We were overcome with relief when the tests showed that I had a rare inbuilt immunity to German measles. However, we were both aware of the miscarriages I had previously and that it was difficult for me to carry a pregnancy to full term. Now we were expecting twins. We were poor and our future uncertain. There was no way of predicting how we would manage financially. Yew Teng had a way of bringing joy and humour into our daily life and helped put our difficulties in perspective as we prioritized and managed them in stages. All he wanted to do for the moment was to take care of me. He accompanied and waited for me at every hospital visit. Whenever I woke up in pain as four elbows and four knees pushed and kicked to create more space in my small frame, Yew Teng was there to hold me. When I was on bed rest for a month in the final stages of the pregnancy, Yew Teng cooked the most nourishing meals for me using his father's recipes. I was glowing when it was time for our children to be born.

On 25 January 1978, I gave birth to my twin daughters, and named them Lilianne (after my two aunts, Lily and Anne) and Pauline (after my Uncle Paul). It was one of the coldest winters in decades and Cambridge was blanketed with snow. But the sun that blazed down from the sky that day made the snow-covered courtyard of the maternity hospital glisten like a constellation of stars. Becoming a mother transformed me profoundly—I had brought two beautiful beings into this world, I was their source of life, protector, and playmate. My children were the centre of my life and being around them was my greatest joy. They were precious beings, and all I wanted was to provide them with the most nourishing home I could and help them grow up to be confident, creative and centred. Yew Teng was a wonderfully loving father, he was relaxed and natural with the children. When spring arrived, we would put our daughters in the twin pram and go on walks to the Cambridge Botanical Garden or along the Cam River to Grantchester. We would lie on the grass and the babies would crawl all over him. Whenever possible, he would spend hours in the second-hand bookshops, then relax in a sarong when he returned home, and play affectionately with our children, whistling his favourite songs to them.

Motherhood made me redefine my priorities. I realized that I needed to shape my life in a way that I could nurture my daughters and provide them with a loving and enriching home. The only way I could do this was to find a stable job and source of income. I could no longer lead my life according to abstract intellectual idealism. I had to find a way to apply my idealism in practical terms, to try to make a decent living even as I was trying to change the world. Yew Teng never focused much on financial stability or accumulating material wealth. He found a way of being happy with whatever he had as he focused on his vision and the purpose of life. To him, living your principles was the most important, and he had faith that somehow things would work themselves out. He influenced me with this mindset and we spent long evenings together, as he smoked his pipe and talked about world affairs—how to be effective in shaping a fairer world through social and political actions—and how to just live. He taught me not to take myself and problems too seriously, and to laugh and enjoy simplicity. He had a way of making me feel emotionally secure, free, and beautiful. But, even as I was carried by his energy, I knew that I could not rely on him for much of the practical parts of life. From my childhood experiences, I knew that without some financial security, there would be tensions and unmet needs that could derail relationships and even destroy family bonds. I, therefore, had to get back to my feet to find a profession that could support our children and the two of us.

In 1979, I began my career in academia at IDS after completing my PhD. It was here that I started finding ways to work professionally on the issues I cared about. When I joined IDS, it was one of the world's leading centres of international development thinking and practice, under the directorship of Professor Richard Jolly. The institute applied its rigorous academic skills to understand and address the complexities of the post–colonial world and its development agendas. I was exposed to the development strategies promoted by IDS. It identified poverty reduction, job-led growth, and inequality as national priorities of new nations that required urgent international development action and support. Pioneers like Professors Dudley Seers, Hans Singer, and Richard Jolly were among the first to stress the importance of aligning education with employment in newly independent states to reduce widespread social frustrations, especially among the unemployed youth. They led the World Employment Missions of the International Labour Organization (ILO). Their Kenyan mission, in particular, had a big impact on development thinking in the 1970s by focusing on the need to address precarious work in 'the informal sector' and 'redistribution with growth'.

Many of these issues were examined from a gender perspective in the Women and Development Programme headed by Dr Kate Young, which I was part of during my time at IDS. My focus was on women, migration, and 'the informal sector', on making the world of work more equal and secure for women since they held poor-quality jobs at the lower echelons of the occupational ladder. In particular, I explored my earlier interest on ways to improve the quality of women's employment to ensure decent earnings that can support their lives and change women subsidizing the economy through unpaid or undervalued work.

The programme brought together female scholars and practitioners with different perspectives from various parts of the world. It provided the space to interact with people like Lourdes Beneria, a Spanish–American economist who eventually became Professor Emerita at Cornell University. When I met her, she was working on labour economics, women's work, and the informal sector at the World Employment Programme of the ILO. We worked well together and she soon published my earlier work on migrant women workers in her volume, *Women and Development*, published in 1982. It was also at IDS that I concentrated on academic writing and eventually published my first book entitled *Working Women in South-East Asia*. Several articles followed, including 'Asian Women Wage-Earners' in the *World Development* journal.

Contesting Feminisms

My time at IDS was not without its struggles. It was the beginning of serious feminist discourse globally, an important time for female scholars to define research agendas and sharpen their own thinking on pivotal questions that preoccupied them. The IDS provided us the space for mutual learning and exploring how the larger development agenda could be impacted by women's agendas for change. We were pushed to think and rethink critical issues and challenge ourselves to go beyond our comfort zones. I had to navigate through the labyrinth of ideas in my encounters with radical Western feminist thinkers.

I realized that there were several contesting forms of feminisms, rooted in divergent approaches and analysis. Many radical Western feminists, up to the mid-1980s, took a very critical approach to motherhood and regarded the rejection of motherhood as a pre-requisite for overcoming women's subordination and gaining equality. I found that their definition of feminism did not necessarily reflect my own experience and understanding. Motherhood had immeasurably enriched my life, and when I thought of the struggles and resilience of my own mother and grandmother, I saw them as women who were caught in unequal economic and social systems, not as victims of an abstract patriarchy who were further oppressed by motherhood. In my research at IDS, I focused more on how vulnerable employment, with little social protection, and the undervalued work of women were built into economic and social systems that reinforced each other, and how these systems needed to change.

At IDS, articulating my thoughts was more than an academic pursuit. I was aware that my research and writing could contribute to the direction of thinking that affected women in the developing world. I immersed myself in the process of discovering my own voice, defining my own thoughts, and asserting my position. This did not come easily to me. I had to clarify my own thoughts and find the mental strength and courage to speak and engage with powerful voices and personalities on a professional basis. Realizing that the intellectual friction I felt with radical Western feminists originated from our different experiences and contexts, I listened respectfully and navigated differences in opinions to find a common cause where possible, but learned to shape discussions to reflect the complex realities of women from the developing world.

While struggling to formulate my thoughts and intellectual frameworks, I drew immensely from the pages of history and the social realities that I witnessed growing up. In particular, I was urged by the lives of the women who surrounded me as a child—my grandmother, my mother, my aunts, and the women in my neighbourhood who escaped their feudal–patriarchal society. They were all strong and formidable women, but many endured economic and social hardships that distorted their lives and deprived them of freedom to reach the lives they might have imagined due to the economic and social arrangements that damaged their possibilities.

Another strongly held position by several feminist scholars at that time was regarding the relationship between women and men as the main site of struggle. This clear-cut gender dichotomy was not something I could concur with. I had been surrounded by supportive men—my uncle, my husband, my brother, and many male friends, all of whom had helped me break gender barriers. For me, it was far more complex. In my understanding and experience, the sites of struggle to transform lives and remake societies—especially those coming out of the Cold War, colonialism, and entrenched patriarchal structures—were political, social, and economic power relationships. Imperialism and colonialism, structures discriminating against women, and totalitarian regimes intolerant of diversity and equal citizenship rights were all systems of power that have shaped our world and created major barriers to human freedom and agency. These forces of historical racism and gender discrimination were systems of exclusion and structures of life that caused deep human suffering for both men and women, albeit differently and differentiated by class, caste, ethnicity, and varied histories.

After studying various theories as well as reflecting on lived experience, I came to understand that gender discrimination affects both men and women, and shapes the dynamics in our societies, our institutions, and households. I realized that men with power have shaped our world and institutions and, generally, men regard themselves as more entitled and privileged socially. But they are also trapped in pre-defined masculinity. As part of their manhood and identity, they are recruited to fight and die in wars; and expected to be stronger, have less emotions, more power over the external world, and more authority to control; and be the decision-makers and economic provider of families. Some bring their experience of humiliation and violence into their relationships and tear their homes or themselves apart when their hurt egos perceive their masculinity and power challenged or their status destroyed. I have witnessed broken men, the unravelling of family relationships and individual lives when men become jobless. After my father lost his source of livelihood, I saw the way he lived a life of illusions to hide his humiliation and shattered dreams. What history had he internalized that turned him violent? I will always have questions about him that have no answers.

Most women have had to struggle with systemic gender discrimination in both public and private spheres. This has devastated lives through multiple forms of violence, the devaluation of women's work and creativity, and the erosion of women's legal rights and voices in decision-making. Many women are expected, to accept the way they are treated and valued—to normalize the violence, their subordinated roles, and diminished selves. Yet, many women even in the worst circumstances refuse to submit to discrimination and find ways of overcoming it.

Generations of female pioneers around the world have resisted systems of gender discrimination, breaking 'unbreakable' barriers to achieve equal rights and dignity for women. They have taken to the front lines of change to get women the right to vote, decent working conditions, quality education, and break the cycle of abuse. They have provided leadership to undo the damage caused by gender inequality and to reshape our world so that women would no longer be undernourished, undervalued, undereducated, overworked, and underpaid. However, gender inequality, entrenched in structures, norms, and practices, makes it difficult for women alone to dismantle discriminatory policies and power that devours human freedom and dignity.

For me, humanity's progress requires us to break out of understanding our world in terms of rigid divisions and categories. It has to be about understanding how power is unequally distributed and used, and how, historically, women have experienced patriarchal power and institutions. It is about building alliances for societal change that search for better ways of living and relating, recognizing the destructive impact of gender discrimination on both men and women. This involves balancing power by transforming the economic, social, and political situation of women, empowering them to cocreate societies where both women and men are equally respected and can flourish to their full human potential.

My encounters with diverse female scholars from around the world made me appreciate IDS as an institution, providing the intellectual environment to explore and respect different perspectives that were often politically difficult in our own countries. We identified common struggles and shared concerns but also issues reflecting diverse experiences that had to be worked out separately to effectively shape our different development trajectories. As an intellectual centre of excellence, the IDS valued debates that generated new thinking and encouraged the diverse contributions of academia from the developing world to better advise development policy and practice. My thinking was appreciated, and I was soon invited to major international gatherings and found my writing on reading lists of several universities. The analytical framework and approaches that I developed in the IDS guided my career directions for many years, as the global women's movement worked to weaken the grip of gender discrimination and help remake our world to be what it can be.

Politics and Development

By the early eighties, the survival of the IDS itself, however, came under threat with the changing political climate of the United Kingdom and the world. The institution and the staff had to navigate major shifts in British politics and in the focus of development studies following the election of Margaret Thatcher in 1979. Much of the IDS's approach to development was questioned, its funding was cut, and it was undermined.

The global economy and the developed economies of Western countries were badly affected by the oil crises of the 1970s when Arab oil producers dramatically raised world oil prices and imposed an embargo and the Iranian Revolution interrupted oil exports. These actions generated unprecedented financial wealth for the oil-producing countries of the Middle East. However, the embargo and the sudden increase in oil prices caused a major global shock and the collapse of the stock market. They triggered high unemployment and stagnant growth with soaring inflation—termed stagflation in the developed economies. Trade unions in Britain demanded higher wages due to rising prices and organized widespread strikes and disruption of services in 1978-79, during the coldest winter in sixteen years. All of this ultimately led to the fall of the Labour government. With the new Conservative government, emphasis was placed on drastic changes to trade union laws, neoliberal economic policies and structural adjustment to cope with rising debts and deficits in the developing world, and stagnant growth and 'unsustainable financial burdens' in the developed countries.

With the refocusing of development, and emergence of hardline policies on immigration and the employment of foreign expertise, I was told that, as a foreigner, my contract would not be renewed. Returning from Singapore after one of my meetings abroad, I was detained at the immigration for several hours with one of my daughters, who was just over a year old. The legitimacy of my employment status was questioned and, being a weekend, it took hours to locate someone from the IDS to verify the situation. My baby was hungry, and I was reprimanded when I asked for a clean nappy for her.

My detention at immigration coincided with the time of the Iranian Revolution. There were several young Iranian women in the area with me. I could hear them crying and begging to stay, describing threats to their security at home. I heard their screams as they were forcefully dragged back to the plane. I felt so helpless, wishing I could stop the deportation and hear their stories to understand what they were escaping from. The image stayed in my mind and I wondered about the nature of this revolution and its impact on women's lives. I hoped with all my heart that I would never find myself in such a heartbreaking situation and hoped even more that our countries would not be destabilized or become intolerant and violent resulting in forced displacement.

The shift in British politics started the unravelling of the post-war consensus of the 'welfare state', with the lowering of government spending on social safety nets and the privatization of public services to reduce public debt and budget deficits. Development experts at the IDS intervened, concerned that the new political regime would pressure multilateral institutions to make this 'structural adjustment' their approach to development with devastating impact on poor countries. I knew there would be serious consequences of the budget cuts on social protection for low-income women and their children in the developed countries as well, based on my personal experience with the British healthcare system.

The National Health System (NHS) had been there for me during the 1978 Winter of Discontent[10] when I was going through a difficult pregnancy. Despite the widespread workers' strikes during the coldest winter in two decades, the nurses at the Cambridge Maternity Hospital provided the best possible care when I needed it the most. The doctors and specialists gave the same quality of care, provided for free to all the fifteen British

---

[10] The Winter of Discontent refers to the winter of 1978–79 in the United Kingdom, which was marked by a series of nationwide strikes by trade unions against the then Labour government's attempt to impose an income policy to curtail wage increases.

women with whom I shared the ward while on bed rest for a month. The NHS enabled me to have healthy twin daughters against many odds—a gratitude I will remember for life. For me, it was an intimate experience of how social democracy, the 'Third Way', delivered much better social support than other systems I knew. Ordinary people were cared for, and this would be eroded under the banner of austerity.

A global community of support grew to address the financing for development and the challenge of redesigning macroeconomic policies to ensure quality education, healthcare, and employment for all, based on fiscal sustainability and a viable economic strategy. Many of us argued that instead of damaging cuts to effective social programmes that provided benefits and social protection to low-income communities and households, more could be done to explore sustainable arrangements, the respective roles of the market and the state, and innovative financing for social protection and services. Ideas like the Tobin tax on currency transaction were already suggested in 1972 together with addressing corruption and tax evasion, improving the tax base, and progressive taxation. Our position was clear—social concerns could not be thrust to one side. Social protection built people's resilience against vulnerability, helping them get to their feet when they fell. Social spending had to be regarded as investment linked to economic growth and human development, bringing greater income security and social stability to all.

As many at the IDS had feared, in the poorer countries of Africa and Latin America, the first generation economic adjustment programmes to deal with mounting debts and deficits resulted in the 'lost development decade' of the 1980s as several countries fell deeper into poverty and hopelessness. In his 1981 'State of the World's Children' report, James Grant, the Executive Director of the UNICEF warned: 'Not for a generation have expectations of world development, and hopes for an end to life-denying mass poverty, been at such a low ebb.'

According to the UNICEF, in thirty-seven of the poorest countries of the world, spending on health fell by 50 per cent, and with the overwhelming of fragile healthcare systems, they saw increases in maternal and child mortality and falling life expectancy. The caregiving burden of women increased exponentially, as the state abdicated responsibility; many women were forced to leave their income-earning work. The HIV/AIDs epidemic in Africa exacerbated the situation, as the medical crisis turned into a socio-economic crisis and a human tragedy. People needed healthcare, education, livelihood support, and social services more badly than ever.

Transnational religious groups, including from the oil-rich Middle East, with their various ideologies and agendas quickly filled the vacuum, providing social support on the ground with local partners when the state or traditional development partners withdrew. This breaking of 'the social contract' between states and citizens had consequences years later. It led to the growing mistrust of state institutions accompanied by stronger allegiances to non-state actors who often emphasized religious or ethnic identities in the delivery of services. Leading economist, Professor Richard Jolly, then with UNICEF, knew this and worked against the stream to urgently shift the focus of the international community and multilateral system back to human development with his book *Structural Adjustment with a Human Face*. With many developing countries facing severe debt problems, structural adjustment programmes (SAPs) were introduced by the International Monetary Fund (IMF) and the World Bank as conditions for receiving loans. These adjustments involved cuts to education, healthcare, and social services, resulting in severe human costs as explained in the book. *Structural Adjustment with a Human Face* presented a need for an alternative approach, encouraging the International Monetary Fund and the World Bank to give greater attention to poverty and human concerns in designing their structural adjustment programmes.

Return to Asia

Just as my contract was coming to its end at the IDS, ESCAP in Bangkok offered me a job to assist with youth unemployment and youth development in Asia, after hearing me speak at one of the international conferences in New Delhi. I gladly accepted, full of enthusiasm and idealism, and travelled there in January 1982 with my daughters just before their fourth birthday. Yew Teng stayed behind in Brighton; he promised to join us as soon as he could find a way of doing so without flying. We waited for six months for him to tie up the loose ends in England and travel by sea to South East Asia. I knew it was as difficult for him as it was for us, especially with limited financial resources. For these six months, I was a single parent, working full-time; I had to find accommodation and a school for the twins, and someone to care for them while I was away at work. Yew Teng's father and one of my aunts came to help us for the first month as I got organized. Instead of being frustrated with Yew Teng's absence, I decided to create an enriching life for my children immediately. I hired a driver who drove us out of Bangkok on weekends— to the mountains of Khao Yai so the girls could play with the elephants and deer and be with nature, to stay overnight at a horse farm in Kanchanaburi, and to the seaside of Hua Hin to play with the waves and feel the sand. When Yew Teng finally reached Bangkok, he joined the life we had created.

Historically, the UN economic commissions are its regional intergovernmental platforms for decision-making and cooperation to address development challenges facing a particular region. They played strong roles in the socio-economic and political assessments and policy directions of post-war Europe and Asia. In fact, in the fifties, the Economic Commission for Asia had invited and worked closely with Gunnar Myrdal, the head of the Economic Commission for Europe, to produce *Asian Drama: An Inquiry into the Poverty of Nations*, a book in three volumes that was the result of Professor Myrdal's 10-year study of poverty in Asia. Published in 1968, the book captured the 'human drama and the desperate strivings for national consolidation and economic development in South Asia'. I had been inspired as a student by my encounter with Professor Myrdal during my European voyage, and I cherished the copy of his masterwork that he had gifted to me. Professor Myrdal's approach guided me in my work, particularly his insistence that economic problems must be studied in 'their mutual relationships' in demographic, social, and political contexts. I was full of hope, glad to return to Asia with the opportunity to devote myself working for the region. However, I was totally unprepared for what awaited me. ESCAP had fallen from its peak of excellence and purpose. I had to navigate a bureaucracy that was built on the best ideals of the UN Charter to promote 'better standards of life in larger freedom', but had been captured by men with agendas that I found unworthy of the UN.

There were many things I expected from the UN after my rich exposure to the IDS and the ILO, and inspired by people like Gunnar Myrdal. Instead, the institution that was supposed to work for our future, uphold women's dignity, and inspire our youth had been compromised. The male leadership in the section I worked had turned the working culture toxic. There was widespread abuse of the duty-free privileges to bring in imported cars. I was asked to use my privilege and name to import an

expensive car tax-free for a local elite in return for compensation.
I refused and got myself a second-hand car instead to the great
annoyance of the people involved. They warned me that I would
be punished when the time came to sell it. Because of the control
by the syndicate operating in the organization, they said that no
one would dare buy my car and it would land in the Chao Phraya
River. I was deeply disappointed that this institution, which
had been established to advance public interest, was being used
to secure the vested interests of a few. I saw how its values were
betrayed because of the unchecked power of a network of men
engaged in corruption for their personal gains.

Worse than this corrupt practice was the unfiltered misogyny
in the organization. Sexual harassment was rampant. My faith in
the organization collapsed when I witnessed how sexual servicing
was negotiated with development partners and incorporated
regularly into professional missions. With two young children,
and as the main earning member of my family, I did not have the
luxury to resign and walk away immediately. I had to find ways
of interacting with integrity. The tension was too much, and, for
the first time in my life, I developed severe earaches, which I felt
was a psychosomatic reaction from listening to doublespeak. This
happened when I discovered a complex web of deception and
lies in the workings of the Youth and Development Division. At
their official UN conferences, the officials involved spoke about
the importance of youth as future ethical leaders. As far as they
were concerned, these were just empty words and professional
rituals. When the official programme ended, some of the youth
participants, who were almost all men, were taken to experience
'entertainment' and engage with young women in the 'hospitality
industry'. The tension between what was expected in cultivating
UN values in our youth and the reality of their corruption was too
much to hear and bear.

I confided in the most respected female colleague in the division, Daw Aye from Burma, who was in charge of the regional programme of the United Nations Voluntary Fund for Women that later became the United Nations Development Fund for Women (UNIFEM). She told me that most people, including in authorities, knew about what was happening, and advised me to see a doctor, concentrate on my work, and not try to take the system on. I could not comprehend her words until years later when I met a Singaporean UN official in New York who had worked for the organization in Bangkok, managing the duty-free programme for the staff. Yeo Bock Cheng described to me, and later in his chapter of an edited book by Professor Tommy Koh[11], how he was instrumental in 'nipping in the bud a number of dubious schemes'. For this, he was 'abducted at gunpoint' by a former staff member and an accomplice and was targeted to be killed. His family was also threatened. Eventually, he was robbed, beaten up, and abandoned 'in a paddy field far out of town'. This happened in early 1978, four years before I joined the organization.

Although I did not know the persistence and depth of the problem, I had already started preparing for my exit. To my surprise, there was an unexpected break in the dark clouds as competent women were recruited into senior positions—as directors of the division—to give credibility to the institution. Their leadership changed the dynamics of the workplace and enabled middle-level professionals like me to serve more seriously. Elizabeth Reid was appointed temporary director of the whole division. She was the first adviser on women's affairs to Australian

---

11   Yeo Bock Cheng, 'The United Nations—A Personal Experience', in *50 Years of Singapore and the United Nations*, ed. Tommy Koh et al. (Singapore: World Scientific, 2015), pp. 302–09.

Prime Minister Gough Whitlam, and the founding director of
the United Nations Asia and Pacific Centre for Women and
Development (APCWD) in Tehran from 1977 to 1979. This
centre, established at the first United Nations World Conference
on Women in Mexico in 1975, was shut down during the
Iranian Revolution. Elizabeth was in between assignments after
working as principal officer in the United Nations Secretariat
for the 1980 World Conference of the Decade for Women. We
instantly connected and eventually became close. I felt in tune
with Elizabeth because of her resilience, determination, and deep
involvement with the women's movement. Her feminism aligned
closely with mine, concerned with the restructuring of society for
greater equality. We were both interested in using our institutions
as a vehicle to advance women's rights and opportunities.
Elizabeth was a leader who knew how to navigate a bureaucracy
that was hostile to women and worked to make its structures more
responsive to women's needs. As a young female professional, I
used the opportunity of her leadership to highlight a serious, but
silent, issue in Asia. I prepared the first intergovernmental paper
that addressed the trafficking of young women and girls in Asia as
a development and human rights concern, moving the focus away
from criminalizing the victims.

The migration and trafficking of young women, for the sex
industry in particular, were already highly visible in Thailand,
as the country became the most popular 'rest and recreation'
destination for soldiers during the Vietnam War. The trade in
female sexuality had become big business during the Cold War
and many young women were said to be 'recruited voluntarily'
as 'hospitality girls' into this 'entertainment industry'. However,
there was a hidden issue that no government wanted to talk about.
Throughout South and South East Asia, according to a 1975 UN
estimate, almost forty-two million children under the age of 15

were working illegally, bonded in 'the unlicensed sector'. Young girls from poverty-stricken areas were coerced from the child labour market into the brothels.

I wanted our governments to take human trafficking of women and children seriously and find ways of addressing the social inequalities, development, and human rights aspects of the problem. For a while, no government attending the ESCAP Intergovernmental Committee Meeting on Social Development wanted to be the first speaker to address the issues in the background paper. There was five minutes of embarrassing silence, after which, various governments, led by the Philippines, discussed the issue and endorsed the analysis and recommendations. The initiative was highly appreciated by the United Nations Economic and Social Council (ECOSOC) and they incorporated the issue into their global agenda. It was at this time that Elizabeth's short appointment came to an end. While I was sad to see her go, I was pleased that another competent woman was appointed to the same leadership position. Dr Nancy Viviani, another highly respected adviser to the Whitlam government, took over the helm of the Social Development Division of ESCAP on the eve of the regional preparatory process for the UN Third World Conference on Women. Working her way out of the institutional mess she inherited, she quickly assigned me to work on issues that the conference should examine from the Asia-Pacific perspective.

I focused on two areas that were impacting women's lives and possibilities—the use of culture and religion as political ideology and women's work in the informal sector. The first issue included discussions on the Iranian Revolution and its impact on women— remembering the women who were deported from the London airport. This got ESCAP and me into trouble, as the Iranian Government widely objected to the intergovernmental paper. Nancy was caught off guard and asked how I had managed to get such a paper into the intergovernmental agenda. Unfortunately, at that time ESCAP acted more as a conference-servicing entity with no one paying much attention to the substance of any paper. I was new, having just come out of an academic environment where debates generated discussions and policy decisions, and had expected the same from a UN intergovernmental debate. I was surprised when the head of the Australian delegation to the meeting told Nancy that ESCAP had never addressed cultural issues before. Nancy called me a 'Young Turk' for sparking controversy, although she did not totally disapprove of me surfacing the issue.

It was to the credit of Shah A.M.S. Kibria, the executive secretary of ESCAP (1981–92) and former finance minister of Bangladesh, that the controversy was finally put to rest. Mr Kibria was regarded as a strict and experienced leader brought in to dismantle the earlier corruption and reform the organization. He left a deep impression on me when he came down to the division and asked to meet with the young woman responsible for the political uproar. His words still echo through my ears: 'If women are affected when culture and religion are introduced as ideology, let us investigate it. When VAW destroys lives, let us address it.' It was a short meeting. Soon, I not only kept my earlier permanent UN contract, but was also recommended for accelerated promotion. The organization appreciated my capacity to face criticism with self-conviction and the courage to stay the course. It was with great sadness that I learned that Mr. Kibria was assassinated in Bangladesh in 2005 for his principles and political beliefs.

I tried my best to find or create meaningful projects in ESCAP that I could do with integrity, as the organization provided great job security with generous benefits, especially for the education of my children. Yet, I was unhappy and unfulfilled, and had to escape from the corruption and the work culture that were making me ill. Towards the end, I decided that the rewards of the security offered were not enough to recharge my spirit and enthusiasm. I was desperate to find a way of both supporting my children and being wholesome.

In the midst of all this, the APCWD shifted to Bangkok from Tehran after it was shut down during the Iranian Revolution. It was one of the four regional institutions recommended for merger as part of the UN reform. The Rector of the United Nations University, Soedjatmoko of Indonesia, conceptualized a new and innovative development think tank 'far enough from the governments to be independent but near enough to be trusted' for its knowledge and analysis. The new entity, the Asian and Pacific Development Centre (APDC) was to lose its UN status and become an intergovernmental organization based in Kuala Lumpur, Malaysia. There was an exodus of UN staff who felt insecure with the new arrangements and significantly reduced salaries and benefits. The newly appointed executive director of APDC, Dr Mohd Shahari Ahmad Jabar from Malaysia, was present at the 1983 and 1984 ESCAP sessions to finalize the details of the transfer and the work programme. He heard me speak at one of the sessions and approached me to head the APCWD as it became the Women and Development Program of the Asia Pacific Development Centre. I negotiated very hard, telling him that I had a permanent UN contract. What he was offering was a one-year contract in a new centre where the funding was not secure. I told him that I would consider it on one condition—that I have full autonomy over my programme direction and control over the additional resources I raise. He quickly agreed and I had a few days to decide.

When I finally handed in my letter of resignation to ESCAP in June 1984, the director of human resources refused to accept it and asked me to see him urgently. He said that I was 'jumping from the frying pan to a sinking ship'. Nancy Viviani was outraged when I informed her of my decision to leave. She felt that her staff had 'been poached' without a warning from the APDC executive director. It was a very difficult choice for me as a young mother and the main breadwinner of the family, but I remained confident in the choice I had made. Neither did I worry about what people around me said, nor did I underestimate the challenges ahead of me, including working and nurturing my six-year-old twins on a one-year contract in a country where Yew Teng was a highly visible opposition leader. However, even with all the security that ESCAP offered, I could not ignore the dominant work culture entrenched in the system despite the emergence of better leadership. Nor could I remain passionate about preparing documents for intergovernmental discussions that I felt were often not taken seriously and, therefore, had little impact on people's actual lives. The reform of ESCAP had started, but it was not what I wanted to spend my youthful, impatient energy on. Eventually, Nancy understood.

And so, I left the security of a permanent contract with the UN and took on a job with far less certainty. It turned out to be one of the best decisions I made in my early career, for it was a job that offered far more possibility for creating the kind of change that I believed would make real difference in the lives of women in developing countries. It was also the job through which I learned to become a leader.

First woman to head ESCAP, appointed by UNSG Ban Ki-moon, 2007

Noeleen with Amartya Sen in Oxford, 2018

Noeleen with Yew Teng in Salzburg, 1970

With women leaders working on mediation — Former Presidents Tarja Halonen of Finland and Michelle Bachelet of Chile, Former Foreign Minster Asha Rose Migiro of Tanzania — in Helsinki, 2018

With UNSG Kofi Annan and UNDP Administrator Gus Speth at the General
Assembly, New York, 1999

Visiting Aung San Suu Kyi at her home after her release from house arrest, 2011

With ASEAN SG, Surin Pitsuwan, visiting Cyclone Nargis affected communities in Myanmar, 2008

With Hillary Clinton and Ela Bhatt at the UN Fourth World Conference on Women in Beijing, 1995

With PM of Bangladesh Sheik Hasina, PM of Korea Chung Un-chan, and President of Kiribati Anote Tong at ESCAP's 66th Commission in Incheon, 2010

With Lilianne in Venice, 2012

With Pauline in Salzburg, 2011

With Timorese women in Mauxiga, Timor-Leste, 2002

With displaced women and children in Afghanistan, 2002

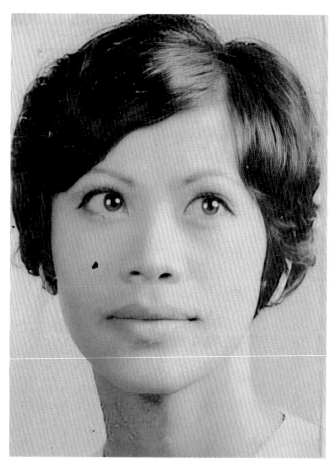

Young Noeleen in Siglap, Singapore, 1962

4

Empowerment at the Margins

'Women are the inheritors and guardians of the "padi pun", the sacred rice with the spirit that renews the cycle of our harvest and our being.'

—*Iban Woman Elder*

It was a difficult balancing act, walking the tightrope of my new reality. I left the security of the United Nations so that I could reimagine the world and dream again. But all the while, the well-being of my family remained at the top of my priorities. I had a clear sense of purpose, of what I wanted to do and how I wanted to contribute to the world. But at the same time, I was nervous, not knowing how I was going to pull everything together on a one-year contract, with the twins being so young, and with Yew Teng being an established opposition leader who believed that one had to always stick to principles in the toxic world of politics. In the face of these uncertainties, I buried my fears and decided to fully concentrate on creating a meaningful and vital programme for the Asia-Pacific region.

I wanted to use my leadership to harness the power of institutions to make a real difference to the lives of people at the margins. The APDC in Kuala Lumpur provided me the platform to reach out to marginalized communities, researchers, and decision-makers in the region and facilitate their dynamic interactions to respond to concrete development challenges. As an intergovernmental organization, the centre had the mandate and legitimacy to bring governments and their bureaucracies closer to vulnerable people.

There was no shortcut to success in APDC. It was a new regional development centre and our job was to position it for success. Dr Shahari, the executive director, managed to recruit eight senior professionals to be his programme directors. Most were development experts frustrated with dysfunctional international and national bureaucracies, and all were given the freedom to experiment, innovate, and break barriers. I was the only woman among my seven male colleagues and their senior staff, but we all worked well as a team. We accepted our shared responsibility to work together with unity of vision and direction by assisting member states to shape a balanced and fairer economic and social order for our people.

I drew inspiration from the IDS model of a development centre, from the different thinkers and reformers who had influenced me, but I also searched for new development approaches that the mandate of the APDC offered for Asia. The APDC was located in a region of great diversity and change, positioned as a network organization for regional cooperation and the sharing of development thinking, strategies, and practice. Its work focused on rural development and poverty reduction, industrial development, public policy and management, energy and development, and women and development. My responsibility was to ensure that women benefited from the social and economic advancements in their societies. I knew there was much work to be done to transform the dominant models of development if women were to truly benefit from them. It would require confronting barriers that held women back in both public and private spheres; charting gender inequality in legal, social, and economic rights; and revealing how women were treated and valued in their society based on ethnicity, class, and geography. It would mean changing the practices that predominantly focused on the realities of men and kept making women's experiences irrelevant.

Transforming Mainstream Development

The discussions and analysis I had been exposed to in the Democratic Socialist Club (DSC), during my European trip as a student to discover the 'middle way', as well as my time in Cambridge and Sussex, were now all playing out in real life. I realized that new nations in Asia were searching for drivers of development that could generate new prosperity, reduce poverty, and establish better standards of life for their citizens. Achieving rapid economic growth became the region's principal development paradigm. From my studies, I understood that countries were looking to generate economic growth through developing their natural resources, human resources, capital investment, and technological capacities, and that they were searching for governance systems that would support these priorities. Countries were balancing the economic and social consequences of democracy, capitalism, socialism, and communism. As a student, I had attended debates about which of these different systems or their creative combinations could best mobilize the talent, energy, and creative capacity of people for the collective effort to create a better life for all. Now, I saw governments struggling to find ways of restructuring social and economic arrangements to achieve their development ambitions and be in control of their own destinies. As an academic at IDS, I had researched how patriarchal structures and forces of historical racism and gender discrimination had built the undervalued work of women into economic and social systems. It was now my opportunity to show how these systems created major barriers to harnessing the talents and agency of women and how they could be changed to benefit all members of society.

The Asia I returned to and worked in as a young professional in the early 1980s was very different from the Asia of my childhood and the 'Asian Drama' captured by Gunnar Myrdal. Emancipation from colonialism had succeeded, and the Vietnam War had finally ended. Countries, from the biggest to the smallest, were breaking out of ideological traps and dogmatism, searching for innovative ways to generate new dynamism in their particular circumstances. It was both fascinating and sometimes heart-breaking to see these struggles play out before me. On my first official trip to China in 1983 while working in ESCAP on youth employment in Asia, I witnessed the early stages of far-reaching reforms under Deng Xiaoping—combining socialism with market-economy, opening China to foreign investment and the global market. On my week-long train ride from Beijing to Guangzhou, getting off to engage with the local communities in several small towns along the way, I witnessed hot debates between the 'socialist roader' and the 'capitalist roader', as they were called in Mao's China. There was a general agreement that China needed 'socialism with Chinese characteristics' to get people out of poverty and become a rising global power. Many women I met were concerned that the shift from the communal system to the household responsibility system, to increase agricultural productivity, was taking place without serious regard to what this would mean for women in terms of their workload. They wanted to know how the economic and social changes could create more opportunities for women. Their concern was, in fact, the central focus of my work in the region.

The rapid economic, political, and social changes taking place across Asia offered tremendous opportunities to create new social arrangements with transformative impact for women, their families, and communities. The region had become the most dynamic in the world and had benefited from a high average rate of economic growth over the past decade. But, I knew from my research and my brief professional experience at ESCAP that there were considerable economic and social imbalances within countries and among countries in different parts of the Asia-Pacific region. Many parts of Asia, especially countries regarded as the 'Asian Miracle', had already made great progress investing in people-centred development, creating middle-class societies by reducing poverty and addressing inequalities through job-led growth, investing in healthcare and education, and building the productive sectors of the real economy. As I studied government and UN reports, I was shocked to find that Asia still accounted for the bulk of the world's deprived people, including more than 60 per cent of those living in extreme poverty. Female illiteracy remained stubbornly high, with girls comprising the majority of out-of-school children and young people. Even in Asia's high-growth economies, women made up the vast majority in low-wage occupations, informal employment, and unpaid work sectors. All these issues had severe consequences for women and girls, and for the society. There was an agreement that far too many people were still left behind and that Asia needed 'development with a human face'. But that face was rarely female. I now had an opportunity to help create an inclusive development paradigm where women mattered.

In every country I visited in my APDC role, I had the opportunity to show that women's participation and leadership would accelerate the economic and social transformation of the region by shifting the mainstream quantity of growth agenda to the quality of growth agenda, improving the quality of life for everyone in more equal and just societies. The way gender discrimination is conceived shapes and determines public policy, research agendas, development practice, and social activism. At APDC, I concentrated on women and girls in urban and rural communities, and the marginalized minorities in remote areas, who were impacted by the various transformations taking place in the Asia-Pacific—industrialization; urbanization and migration; and deforestation, land, and rural development. My research and policy agendas focused on whether the economic arrangements and social environment are empowering or disempowering women in these specific development contexts. We analysed how various development policies and decision-making were impacting women's access to economic and social opportunities, including reward for work, access to productive resources, and equality in law related to women's property and inheritance rights. I wanted to change development practice by pushing the boundaries to improve women's power and voice to influence decisions affecting their lives and communities. I looked at how states and markets could be genuinely transformed to strengthen women's empowerment—ensuring equal access to new opportunities, securing quality employment for women in the region's changing economy, and treating women as people in their own right and not merely as dependents of male heads of households, or instruments for the market or the state.

I argued that effective public policy required both market and state to be mutually reinforcing. Furthermore, good social policies could only be designed if think tanks and decision-makers engaged with real people on the ground, listening to their problems, aspirations and solutions, and to women's perspectives in the diverse development context of the Asia-Pacific. I advocated for women to contribute their insights and participate meaningfully to improve workplace protection, ensure that investment in infrastructure reduces their workload, and empower them to access high-wage sectors as countries undergo transition. With the centre's emphasis on networking, we explored ways of creating meaningful mechanisms to connect women's concerns with policymaking. My programme helped women build their capacity and networks to provide knowledge, seek solutions, and be empowered to influence the development processes affecting them, transforming 'mainstream' economic and social development when it did not work for them.

Building networks linking women across the region as a force for change proved to be hard work. I travelled extensively and invested a lot of time listening to women in the countries I visited, sharing their concerns about life in their communities. From the mountain villages of Nepal and Bhutan to the steppes of Mongolia and Kyrgyzstan, and from the villages of Bangladesh to the islands of the Pacific, I connected with women and their stories, with their aspirations and dreams. I assured them that they could be a force for meaningful change and that they could influence policymaking and government action. They often laughed and were very sceptical, but appreciated how far I had journeyed to be with them instead of just being with the government officials who invited me. With my trusted civil society or local government partners, I crossed rivers and climbed mountains in Nepal to help upscale microfinance programmes for women, walked for hours across the dried lake of Savar in Bangladesh to ensure women's access to the new water and sanitation infrastructure we were building in the village, visited villages around Mount Hagen in Papua New Guinea (PNG) to discuss land issues when there were security concerns. I had many profound exchanges with the women I met on my trips and, although our encounters were often brief, they always deepened my understanding and sense of purpose and energized me in my mission. The women I met always impressed me with their resilience and sometimes surprised me with their gestures of friendship and recognition for my efforts. On my trip to Papua New Guinea, for example, I had helped to prevent women traders from being evicted from the market in East Sepik by negotiating with local officials and convincing them to allow the women to pay for their licences by installment. The next morning, as I was taking a walk on the beach, I saw a group of women approaching me carrying armfuls of garlands made up of seashells and beads. Thinking they were artisans who wanted to sell me their crafts, I smiled and politely declined, until they told me that these were gifts for me to thank me for what I had done for them. 'You have walked many extra miles for us, we will not walk away without thanking you.'

My passion for 'the field' did not go unnoticed. Once at a staff meeting, when directors were asked to share our different approaches to networking, Executive Director Shahari smiled at me and said, 'The only woman in the team and you are so brave! I just locked myself in the hotel at Port Moresby after official engagements when I visited PNG. You went to Mount Hagen and visited all those villages?' I smiled back, not mentioning that I was also with women traders in East Sepik, and even went snorkelling around one of the islands all by myself when I returned to Port Moresby. Building trust, creating belief that change is possible, and mapping strategies for dialogue and engagement with decision-makers were difficult but deeply satisfying when strong bonds of friendship and solidarity were forged. They opened new and wonderful experiences that I would always treasure.

On my visit to Nepal, I was hosted by a very committed government official, Chandni Joshi, who later became my staff at the UN. She wanted me to witness how women were using mountain resources and sustaining the fragile mountain ecosystem—so fundamental to the life of their communities and the whole country. Together with the group that I brought with me, we carefully trekked the steep mountain slopes that were susceptible to landslides to reach the villages at the top. We spent the day listening to the mountain women in these villages describing how they were provided with incentives like microfinance and trained by extension workers to set up cooperatives and use environment-friendly technologies, water collection, and farming practices to support the livelihoods of their families and communities. After a fruitful day, we spent the night at the foot of the Himalayas where we slept outdoors to watch Mars when it was closest to Earth. That night, I watched the stars and the Milky Way and wondered what possibilities existed beyond the stars.

Although the tools to transform development practice available to an intergovernmental institution were limited, with determined leadership it was still possible to carve out a way of working professionally to engage policymakers and empower people at the margins. First, when I presented my programmes at the APDC governing board for approval, I worked to expand the research and policy agendas of governments, convincing them of the importance to address social grievances and exclusion in specific situations. Second, in the implementation of my programmes, I engaged with key decision-makers to value the active participation of vulnerable communities, listen to different narratives, reflect on their concerns and be more responsive to their often 'forgotten citizens'. The third tool I used was designing dialogues for problem-solving and convening decision-makers and the marginalized communities to shape an ongoing conversation about a specific complex problem, like the international migration of domestic workers which I was working on, and embrace evidence-based policy-making. I believed that this practice helped to build social trust so that common grounds and mutually beneficial solutions could be found, and development could be a transformative practice for both the communities and the 'patrons'.

As I engaged with states, academia, and civil society to collaborate and develop meaningful mechanisms for the marginalized communities to impact policy-making on issues that deeply affected them, two areas of work at APDC emerged as the most memorable. The first programme involved indigenous communities, deforestation, and land rights. This issue was especially complex because of the entrenched interests of power and privilege in dealing with our natural world and its resources and with indigenous people. The work required me to have detailed first-hand understanding of the context and its dynamics. It required strategic advocacy, from both inside and outside on decision-making powers to incorporate concerns and ideas from the margins for sustainable economic and social progress. It required years of mobilization from diverse groups to influence political processes to address what it means to live as part of an ecologically interdependent human community.

The second area was the international migration of female domestic workers. We achieved highly significant results by bringing diverse groups together to establish legal frameworks for women's domestic work based on solid research. We created an international network that brought together women's groups, academics, the private sector, and the leadership of President Cory Aquino of the Philippines. We empowered migrant women to contribute their insights and knowledge to our research agenda while helping to frame development issues so that governments could change the policy environment for women's domestic work and safe migration. In doing so, we forged a common regional voice on the care economy and international migration that were emerging on the global agenda.

Indigenous Land Rights and Deforestation

In December 1991, I travelled to Sarawak in East Malaysia to live for two weeks with the Penans, Kelabits, and Ibans along the Limbang River in order to understand first-hand the concerns and dynamics of the communities. Two powerful forces of change were affecting these indigenous communities that I had come to study—the logging of the tropical rainforest by companies who had been given timber concessions and the changes in government policies regarding shifting agriculture and land rights.

Unlike the revenue from petroleum and gas, which was controlled by the Malaysian federal government, states received all logging royalties. Control of timber and land, therefore, lay at the heart of Sarawak's political economy. Historically, most of Sarawak was covered by tropical rainforest, but the pace of logging increased dramatically in the 1980s. In 1984, the year I joined APDC, 5.8 million hectares (three–fifths of the total forest area of Sarawak) were licensed for logging. In 1991 alone, the year I was there, 100,000 cubic metres of timber were logged from the Limbang forest, generating earnings of about RM35 million. In March 1992, when I visited again, the main federal newspaper featured an article in the New Straits Times that stated 'Timber tycoons have become so powerful that removing them would bring down the State government'[12].

The rainforest on which the Penans depended for their survival was becoming increasingly scarce, forcing greater dependency on government programmes to 'bring them out of the jungle'. I stayed with the Penans in Long Napir, the upstream area of the Limbang River together with the academic team I assembled from the local university. The only way to get there was to walk for

---

[12] *New Straits Times*, March 15, 1992.

hours, cross rope bridges, and navigate cliffs with the help of our Penan hosts. I quickly noticed how the widely spread toes on bare feet helped the Penan men move swiftly with greater precision compared with the rest of us. They were hunters and gatherers living in nomadic bands and defined themselves as inhabitants and owners of a foraging range.

Sitting on the mud floor of the camp, I learned that the Penans moved their camps frequently according to game movement and set up camps in areas where their main staple, sago, could be found in abundance. Because of their lifestyle, the Penans acquired minimum material possession and depended on the forest as their guardian and provider. The men hunted away from the camp while the women foraged close to home for vegetables and small game and were in charge of processing the sago. Both complained to me that large-scale deforestation, together with the noise of logging machinery, had driven game deeper into the forest and destroyed important livelihood resources, including sago, building materials, medicinal plants, and muddied their water. The men said they had been offered wage employment and food handouts by the logging companies, but were afraid of the logging machinery—aware of their poor safety record—did not want handouts, and could not bring themselves to participate in the destruction of their own ecosystem. They explained that the natural resource base on which Penan society depended was viewed as communal property and the whole band had a shared obligation to defend territory against encroachment by strangers. Hence, the Penans, both men and women, became increasingly active in resistance and protest movements against the logging companies. Many of them were arrested and imprisoned.

On one of the hunting trips, because they had to go much deeper into the jungle, the men left me in a paddy hut with the Kelabit community in Long Napir. The Kelabits were chiefly shifting agriculturalists. The combination of logging and change in state policies on land rights and shifting cultivation impacted them. I spent hours interacting with the community when they returned from their ladangs (cleared fields), several kilometres away, where they grew hill paddy. The women, with their long bejewelled earlobes, captured my immediate interest and I listened attentively to their stories. They spoke with pride about their relationship with the land and the padi. Their men cleared the forest and transported sago logs and other heavy loads, but the women were in charge of seed selection, the sowing, and weeding. 'We start the new cycle of planting,' they said with pride. Both the men and women worked together in land preparation, harvesting, and threshing. I helped the women with the threshing in the paddy hut, beating bushels of padi to separate the grain from the husk.

The Kelabit men and women both had ownership and user rights to land, although the proportion owned by women was lower. They spoke about their confusion regarding what was happening to their land, and hence to their world. The state government had singled out shifting cultivation rather than logging as the major cause of deforestation and environmental degradation through 'slash and burn'. Consequently, the shifting cultivators in the Limbang region were being pressured by the government to settle and take up permanent cultivation of cash crops such as oil palm, coconut, and pepper in combination with animal husbandry. As state thinking on shifting agriculture changed, there was an increased implementation of the 1979 Land Code Amendment Ordinance, a refinement of the 1958 Land Code that effectively restricted the creation of further customary rights to land. Any party claiming native customary rights to land after 1 January 1958 was now seen to be committing an offence for unlawful occupation of state land. The 1979 amendment broadened the meaning of occupation to include land clearance, ploughing, digging, cultivation and erection of buildings, including huts. The amendment also gave wide powers of arrest, eviction, removal or demolition of implements, buildings, or crops to senior state officials.

Listening to the Kelabits, I realized that changes to land tenure arrangements at the legislative level meant little to them. They could not even read the official notices that were put up. Many who lost their land under these changes were not aware of their loss until they faced prosecution as 'illegals'. Watching an elderly woman stare bleakly out of her hut with despair, it became clear to me that the confusion was too much for some to bear. The Kelabits joined forces with the Penans in protest action, this time against the state.

In comparison to the protest of the upstream communities, the Ibans and the Murats—also known as the Lun Bawang—the midstream shifting cultivator communities reacted differently to the environmental changes. These communities had better access to roads and other infrastructure and services since they were located closer to Limbang town and the Sarawak–Brunei border. This also increased their choices and access to a variety of wage work in the urban areas. I stayed with two longhouse communities—Lun Bawang and Iban. Every household in the two longhouses had at least one able-bodied man working in oil-rich Brunei, mainly as construction workers, returning home about twice a month to renovate their bilik or room. Male outmigration or *bejalai* from these communities was customary, taken as journeys for material profit and social prestige.

From the women and elderly of the various biliks, I learned that, in the past, the bejalai would fit in with the lesser labour demands of the agricultural cycle. With the changes in their environment, this was no longer the case, and women had often been left to fill the vacuum created by male absence. The growth of the money economy, the new economic opportunities open to young men, and the promotion of settled agriculture by the state with changes in land titles registered in the name of male household heads created new gender dynamics in favour of men. The families I interviewed considered their new livelihood system based on stable male wage employment in Brunei at relatively high income, combined with subsistence agriculture, as improving their standard of living. However, the Iban women, especially the elders, lamented their loss of paddy land and the inability to grow their sacred rice as the most dramatic change. They spoke intimately of how their status in the community was intricately bound to being inheritors and guardians of the sacred padi pun[13] that renewed the cycle of community well-being. There was no special status for them in the new arrangements, including in the shift to plantation agriculture. Their authority was severely weakened.

While it was impossible for me to deal with the politics of timber concessions and their impact on customary land rights and the changes they were bringing to the indigenous communities, I saw a possibility to have some influence working with government agencies at the local level that were entrusted to manage and administer land, including 'native customary land'. Local government officials were holding regular dialogues and seminars to gather feedback to ensure effective implementation of government policies on customary land to 'benefit the people'. I realize that 'the people' did not include women and their concerns.

I was able to use my role in APDC to work with the federal and Sarawak state government and their land officials to make some policy adjustments and changes in the practice of registering

---

13   The Ibans conceptualize the padi pun as the soul or spiritual essence of the rice.

land only in the name of male heads of households. Through engagement and gaining the trust of key officials, I was requested to arrange several gender analysis and rigorous gender training workshops through which my team and I were able to change some mindsets and make minor breakthroughs. We used real stories of women from the various communities I visited. The officials could relate to them immediately. Several officials described how, by practice, they immediately excluded any application with a woman's name as she was considered 'a dependent'. They did not realize the implications of their action. After one of my sessions, a senior male government official came up to me and said, 'The discussions made me think of my mother, my grandmother and what they went through.' The next morning, I learned he had a minor heart attack that night and was rushed to the hospital. I was assured there was no connection, but it was dramatic enough for everyone. Soon, I was informed that the sessions helped in the issuing of joint land titles and land ownership for women in female-headed households, restoring some of their security and dignity.

It was especially challenging to address the deforestation concerns of the Penans and the Kelabits at the state level. One of the major contributing factors to the high level of environmental degradation through logging in Sarawak appeared to be a lack of implementation of the forest policy and regulations, despite the fact that a state-level legislative framework for forest protection existed. According to the officials interviewed, the fact that the state minister of environment at that time had a large timber concession in the area made it difficult for junior officers to pursue implementation, given the existing power and social hierarchies combined with the fear of dismissal. They saw themselves as 'small fish' and were not willing to risk their economic security.

We had very little impact locally, and, politically, the federal government had no interest to act. The only alternative was to use the multilateral space provided by the UN to bring governments together to negotiate ground rules that would benefit the whole of society. I hence shifted my focus towards helping to build regional networks of indigenous women lobbying for the respect of the natural world and the dignity of indigenous peoples. We prepared an Asia-Pacific resource book on environment and development, focusing on ideas, actions, and strategies for mobilization and change, and supported indigenous women to engage regionally and connect internationally to voice their grievances and demands during the 1992 UN World Conference on Environment and Development, also known as the Earth Summit. Several important achievements resulted from this Earth Summit. A governmental agreement was reached on the Climate Change Convention that in turn led to the Kyoto Protocol, which entered into force in 2005, and to the Paris Climate Agreement in 2015. For the indigenous women networks, the most important agreement was 'not to carry out any activities on the lands of indigenous peoples that would cause environmental degradation or that would be culturally inappropriate'.

We now know that forests are among the world's most productive land-based ecosystems and are essential for life on earth. They mitigate climate change, conserve biodiversity, provide clean air, and maintain our soil and water systems. There is growing concern that the ecological destruction of our forests, the human encroachment on the habitat of wild animals, and the black market trade in wildlife deplete our biodiversity and even encourage the spread of new and deadly diseases, which can appear when viruses jump species barrier or mutate through climate change. We cannot expect our natural world to provide for us without renewal and care. Today, the UN has a

Strategic Plan for Forests 2017–2030 to halt deforestation and promote sustainable forest management as agreed under the UN Framework Convention on Climate Change (UNFCCC) and the 2030 Agenda for Sustainable Development. There is now global recognition that our forests are global public goods to be sustainably managed for the well-being of the present and future generations.

Tragically, today, nearly 90 per cent of the rainforest in Sarawak has been logged. Could this scale of deforestation and change in land use have been avoided if the indigenous communities were listened to and the natural world was treated as an indispensable ecosystem rather than a commodity? How much of Sarawak's rainforest could have been saved if the authorities had respected human connectedness to nature, if they had appreciated the intimate connection of indigenous women to the forest, their paddy and their land, and if community organizing was not treated as a crime? Could the voracious greed of the powerful, described to me by the local communities whose lives were directly affected, have been stopped in time? Meanwhile, a multibillionaire former Sarawak chief minister, a generous donor to his alma mater—Adelaide University— came under investigation for allegations of bribery and abuse of power[14] by the Malaysian Anti-Corruption Commission that eventually said it was unable to take action, based on available information.[15] Adelaide University has decided to rename the plaza that they had named after him, following a major protest campaign by its students and Australian political and community leaders. In addition, Penan leaders sent a request to the vice chancellor of the University to return the funds received from

14 *The Sydney Morning Herald*, September 8, 2015.
15 *The Star*, March 26, 2019.

him to the indigenous community and conserve the remaining rainforest of Sarawak.

Over a quarter of a century has passed since my first encounter with the Penans, when the power of their organizing showed incipient promise and then got badly thwarted. According to them, they came up against politicians and vested interests using power to enrich themselves, often with impunity at the expense of the indigenous society. But the Penans have bounced back in new ways, and are now part of an international network of indigenous peoples. Today, they continue to defend their customary rights to land and the forest, and recently presented the state government with a detailed map, charting the boundaries of their nomadic range, from foraging areas to burial sites. However, the wounds from decades of eroded trust have yet to be healed.

Migration of Female Domestic Workers

The other major issue that I focused on during my time at APDC was migration and female domestic workers. With the social transformation and uneven economic growth in Asia, there was an increasing demand in the richer countries for domestic work, which was provided largely by migrant women from the poorer countries of the region. It was work that economies, families, and societies depended on to care for children and an ageing population, as middle-class women in high-growth countries entered the workforce, households became smaller, and the caregiving role of the extended family was reduced. In the eighties, there were no adequate policies to address the conditions of domestic work and the safe migration of domestic workers. I wanted to place these issues on the policy agendas of our region to bring about better recognition of domestic work, improve the quality of employment and protection of migrant domestic workers. I realized that these were contemporary challenges that would continue to grow and demand solutions.

Like many working mothers with young children, I depended on domestic help to keep the household going while holding a full-time job. It was challenging to balance the responsibilities of raising a pair of twins and performing at the highest level for my professional career. After returning to Malaysia in 1984, Yew Teng devoted himself working across racial divides towards a more inclusive society that cared for all vulnerable persons and their human rights. To navigate our household through complex politics, we each kept our independence and gave each other the freedom to flourish in our own way.

The only extended family I had in Kuala Lumpur was my aunt, Anne, the former mother provincial of the Convent of the Holy Infant Jesus. Aunty Anne was a great help to me and my family; she looked after the children when I had to travel on work assignments. She was an inspiring woman who had dedicated her life to girls' education and women's leadership and improving the lives of vulnerable and destitute communities, particularly among the Indian estate workers in Malaysia. Besides being an essential source of support for our family, Aunty Anne became my closest confidante and spiritual anchor, and she was like a grandmother to my daughters.

For a while, we had part-time helpers, but eventually decided that we needed full-time help to be able to manage all the daily chores, particularly as my work involved a lot of travel. I was introduced, by a recruitment agency, to Iyah, who was from Indonesia. She was an intelligent, gentle, and kind young woman whom I liked immediately. I was horrified to hear her life story. Iyah was a young mother who wanted to migrate in order to educate her young son, but was too poor to pay the cost of using official channels and legal recruitment. Thus, she migrated illegally, was heavily indebted to her recruiters, and could be deported easily. She arrived by boat to Malaysia on a dark, moonless night. The boat filled with people in a similar situation crossed the Straits of Malacca from Indonesia. Because of the Malaysian navy patrol that night, they were all forced to disembark in the waters miles away from a mangrove swamp near Malacca. Many of the migrants did not know how to swim. The waters that night were rough and the currents too strong. So many, Iyah told me, drowned before reaching the shore. I employed Iyah, paid off all her debts and legalized her work status. She worked with me for ten years while I was with APDC and became a trusted member of my household. Iyah's story drew my attention to the ugly side of the recruitment of domestic workers—the smuggling and trafficking of young women in the region.

By the mid-seventies, there was already a huge influx of migrant workers from Asia who were being pulled to the oil-rich countries of the Middle East, which were undergoing massive physical transformation. The Gulf states, with their new-found oil wealth, in particular, were short of labour that was needed for large-scale construction of luxurious cities, oil industry, and manufacturing and services. From East and South East Asia, workers came from South Korea, Philippines, Indonesia, and Thailand. From South Asia, workers flowed from Bangladesh, India, Pakistan, and Sri Lanka. Young women came to work in the service industries and as domestic workers in households, along with male migrants employed in the construction industry. Some of these migrant workers used official channels while many more migrated illegally, including through smuggling routes.

The phenomenon of large-scale migration, including that of female domestic workers, was not limited to the Middle East. The rapidly emerging economies of Asia, including Hong Kong, Singapore, and Malaysia, were highly dependent on migrant workers as well. In 1991, 90 per cent of the estimated 73,000 foreign domestic workers in Hong Kong came from the Philippines. In Singapore, workers from Philippines, Indonesia, Sri Lanka, and Bangladesh replaced the first wave of Malaysian workers. In Malaysia, by the mid-eighties, official estimates put some 350,000 Indonesians as working illegally in the Peninsular. The Malaysian Trade Union Congress, however, put the estimate of around a million illegal Indonesian workers as more realistic—employed mainly in the expanding agricultural sector and in domestic work.

The overseas employment of women to do 'housework' had become big business, involving millions of workers, billions of dollars, dozens of labour exporting and importing countries, as well as a host of intermediate agencies (such as recruitment agencies, banks, airlines, medical clinics, insurance companies, currency dealers, remittance services and couriers). It had become a transnational trade with a full-blown economic ecosystem benefiting countries, businesses, and families based on undervalued and casualized female labour. Despite it being socially vital work requiring diverse skills, work of the home is commonly regarded as 'housework by housewives'—unpaid domestic work that all women can do instinctively. Employment in domestic service is, therefore, regarded as unskilled, informal work done in the house with little legal protection. Like other 'home-based work' of women, domestic work usually has unregulated working conditions, including irregular hours and tasks.

To address this complex and significant phenomenon affecting so many people, I developed a regional research and action programme named 'The Trade in Domestic Workers'. The objectives were to design frameworks and strategies that could contribute to the long-term welfare of the female migrant workers based on solid research and analysis, and to organize multi-stakeholder dialogues to bring about better regulations and working conditions and safer recruitment and migration for domestic workers. This multi-year programme was fully funded by the Dutch Development Corporation and Foreign Ministry. They appointed Professor Geertje Lycklama from the Institute of Social Studies (ISS) at The Hague to help me with the analysis. A formidable academic, Geertje became the first woman Rector of the ISS at The Hague, a senator in the Netherlands, and a dear friend to me till the end of her life. It was one of my most meaningful experiences of sisterhood and collaboration.

Through the research, we created a vast and intricate network of people with different expertise, including decision-makers, women's groups, human rights lawyers, academics, government officials in charge of overseas employment, and central banks, who could shape the migration processes from sending countries (Philippines, Indonesia, Sri Lanka, and Bangladesh), a transit country (Pakistan) and destination countries (Hong Kong, Malaysia, Singapore, and the Gulf). This network was a source of new ideas and strategies for managing the legal and illegal migration of domestic workers. I had assembled an alliance of people with different skills and spheres of influence, some with real political power, all coalescing around the opportunity to make a change. We undertook a comprehensive analysis of macro and micro processes to map out the maze of complicated and tangled webs of interests that ensnare the domestic worker seeking overseas employment. It was one of the most in-depth attempts to address the issue at the time.

My team and I spent a lot of time connecting and interviewing communities and families in the countries of origin and the destination countries and documented their concerns. Our research revealed a recruitment network that not only spanned the sending and receiving countries but permeated down to the villages and linking them to towns and cities abroad. The young women we interviewed shared how some of them were pressured to migrate to support the family and household, swayed by the promise of a higher salary abroad. They felt the powerful social forces of their kinship and neighbourhood networks to 'make sacrifices for the sake of the family', many becoming the main breadwinner of their families. Daughters and young mothers were persuaded by the recruitment agents to think of the costs involved with migration and overseas employment as an investment, which would subsequently lead to the accumulation of surplus to help their families—a claim that for many might have never materialized. Several women described how difficult it was for them to raise funds for their migration. Most had to do so by selling their assets and taking loans, borrowing, and becoming indebted. Meanwhile, agents conveniently provided loans to cover their fees for the recruitment process through salary deduction. Those who could not cover the full cost of migration were encouraged to use smuggling networks and soon became indebted illegal workers, bonded to their agents.

Our research also mapped the costs and benefits of both sending and destination countries and the migrant worker herself. The benefits tended to be more economic while the costs were primarily social and political. Practically, all countries of origin claimed to have benefited economically, through the remittances of workers. Generally, families also enjoyed the economic impact of domestic worker migration. Income was spent on children's education, improving the family home, on basic necessities as well as more luxurious consumer products, with overall improvement in the standard of living. However, because of salary differentials, the deployment of domestic workers had turned out to be a powerful magnet that drew not only the unemployed and those without professional skills, but also teachers, nurses, and other professionals, whose services were badly needed in their own countries. This constituted a major social cost for the sending countries.

Balancing the costs and benefits, it was clear to us that the international migration of domestic workers would remain, and even increase, in the future, as it was a long-term economic development strategy for both sending and destination countries in our region and for the migrants themselves. Clearly, having public policies in destination countries that addressed the inadequacies in domestic work and provided support to ensure quality services by domestic workers could yield mutual benefits for those who were cared for as much as those who provided care. We, therefore, came up with concrete recommendations and framed them in ways that helped decision-makers understand the urgency for better policies to address the recruitment process and the employment conditions of domestic workers in the region.

The Magic of Mobilization

With our research findings and recommendations, I decided to take urgent action to mobilize the political leadership needed for intergovernmental negotiations to bring about fair and secure living and working conditions for migrant domestic workers. I took courage from my memory of the 'black-and-white amahs' and the authority with which they organized to fix common regulations with employers for their welfare and working conditions. I wanted to go beyond individual employers and negotiate legal frameworks for safe migration and women's domestic work at the highest political level between the countries in our region.

We were fortunate to have in our network Filipina leaders and women's groups in the Philippines with close access to President Corazon 'Cory' Aquino, the first woman to hold the post of

President of the Philippines and the first woman to hold the post of President in Asia. Aquino came into power as the result of the 1986 People Power Revolution that restored democracy to the Philippines after her husband, Senator Benigno Aquino, was assassinated in 1983. Her economic policy centred on restoring economic health and creating a socially responsible economy. She was quick to recognize that migrant domestic workers made valuable contributions to the maintenance of society and economic productivity of both sending and receiving countries. With overseas Filipino worker remittances amounting to $7 billion, and more than 70 per cent of the Filipinos working abroad being women, President Aquino took it upon herself to listen to our concerns and take immediate action. She became our champion. She found a new way of dealing with politics and power, not just to discuss the problem but to come up with decisive policy solutions that made a difference. She was very concerned by our research findings and decided to temporarily ban the deployment of domestic workers on 20 January 1988. The ban was to highlight the need to prevent the abuse and exploitation of female Filipino migrants and to use it to leverage better terms and conditions for the workers. The President appointed an envoy to consult the migrant women's groups, starting with Hong Kong, to renegotiate and enforce government-to-government agreements for better job quality and a fairer deal for Filipino domestic workers.

We facilitated the migrant women to take full advantage of this opportunity since many of the migrant women's groups or those working with them participated in our project. Our network was not only an asset for collaboration to discuss challenges and policy solutions between governments, it also became a meaningful mechanism to support the leadership and engagement of female migrants themselves. It provided the platform for the women to interact, articulate a collective voice, and be speakers in their own right with the policymakers. It allowed them to not just be topics of the discourse but also to voice their grievances, provide recommendations from our evidence-based research, and highlight proposals from the migrant women themselves.

It was a unique opportunity for the mobilization of women's leadership to interact meaningfully with the political economy undergoing rapid change in Asia, to help women create spaces to come together to address and collectively seek solutions to challenges. Our network in the Philippines included dynamic and passionate women who were at the forefront of advocacy on women's rights, some of whom used creative approaches as powerful tools for education and empowerment. Remy Rikken of the Philippine Educational Theatre Association (PETA), for example, used community theatre as a platform for domestic workers to express themselves and grapple with their predicaments. Throughout the country, women were mobilizing around this issue in their own communities and capacities—on the streets, through the media, in the universities, and within institutions of government. Working among these women, I felt the power and the magic of a genuine people's movement that carried the seeds of possibility and found fertile ground for these seeds to grow and flourish. It was a movement that mobilized the collective energy of the grassroots to engage the highest levels of political power.

With intense mobilization by women's groups in the Philippines and political support at the highest level, significant outcomes were achieved. Great importance was placed during renegotiations for destination countries to regulate, standardize, and improve the conditions of domestic employment. Governments of destination countries eventually agreed to abide by standard employment contracts as a way of standardizing terms and conditions of employment, ensuring acceptable working conditions and standards of worker protection. To reduce illegal migration and household indebtedness, there was an agreement for governments of both sending and destination countries to regulate and monitor the activities and exorbitant charges levied by the recruitment agents. The network also helped frame these issues for the bilateral negotiations and facilitated the discussions, as some of the Hong Kong officials were also part of the network and understood the concerns by the time the ban was imposed. Subsequently, President Aquino lifted the ban for selected countries, as they implemented the new agreements and gradually shifted towards greater welfare and better protection of the female migrant workers. The ban for the Middle Eastern countries was the last to be lifted, although the remittances from there were important to the Philippines Government. Today, Filipina domestic workers earn the highest wages among the domestic workers in the region.

Because of the intense women's mobilization programme, major institutional changes also took place within the Philippines itself to recognize and empower the female migrant workers. Migrant workers represented themselves in national and local policymaking bodies. There was greater consciousness that remittances of migrants were a major driver of the country's economy, boosted household income and consumption, and paid for the education of children and siblings and the healthcare of families.[16] Officials of Philippines consulates provided on-site protection to overseas workers, and a welfare fund was established to provide legal assistance, counselling, and emergency loans to stop illegal migration. President Aquino recognized the overseas migrant workers as 'the economic heroes' of the country, acknowledging their contribution to the national economy.

---

[16]   According to the Central Bank of the Philippines, remittances reached $33.5 billion in 2019.

Referring to herself as a homemaker before becoming President, she gave new social status and economic value to women's domestic work.

A key Filipina leader in our network, Dr Patricia Licuanan, chairperson of the National Commission of the Role of Filipino Women, took the lead in working with the Asian Development Bank (ADB) to improve data and statistics on female migrant workers. In 1995, as the chair of the United Nations Commission on the Status of Women, she placed the issue on the agenda of the Fourth World Conference on Women in Beijing (FWCW). Efforts were made in Sri Lanka by network members Savitri Goonesekere, professor of law and later vice chancellor of the University of Colombo, and Radhika Coomarasamy, lawyer and chairperson of the Sri Lanka Human Rights Commission, to develop model contracts for Sri Lankan female migrant workers, with an emphasis on the Middle East. Members of the network also partnered with the Central Bank of Sri Lanka to provide migrant workers a safer and cheaper system of remittances, including by reducing bank charges for the transaction. To establish global norms and standards among countries, leaders, both women and men, engaged with the ILO to set labour standards. This initiated the work towards the UN Convention on Domestic Workers, the legal framework to protect domestic workers that came into force in September 2013. We, at APDC, were proud to be at the heart of a coordinated movement that emerged across Asia to improve the working and living conditions of female migrant domestic workers.

The women who worked on 'The Trade in Domestic Workers' were at the front lines of change, transforming how societies treat domestic work and improving the quality of employment, migration, and security of caregivers. In the process, those who needed care have benefited from better public policies and support. Several of the women in the network have gone on to be regional and global leaders in the multilateral system and ministers of their governments. An evaluation of APDC, commissioned by then UNDP Assistant Administrator Andrew Joseph, the centre's main donor in the nineties, called the Gender and Development programme 'a beacon for the region'.

It was a good time to be at APDC, even on a one-year contract that eventually extended to ten years. It was, essentially, a space where I could experiment with methodologies of research and practice that allowed me to forge intricate networks and cooperation to sustain the dynamism of the region. It was a place from where I could embark on a journey of discovering the countries of Asia-Pacific, to provide strategic assistance for more effective policymaking and institutional-building as the region undertook economic and social transformation to generate inclusive growth. It was a unique opportunity to strengthen the empowerment and agency of women, unleash their potential, and ensure that women benefited from the region's dynamism.

My greatest joy in my role at APDC was having the opportunity to pave a way for working and networking with female leaders at all levels who were powerful decision-makers and game-changers. Together, we were able to exercise a new kind of leadership, one that consistently challenged discrimination, to bring about the needed changes in legal frameworks, policies, and institutions. We became co-creators of a fairer economic and social reality that put vulnerable communities first and empowered people at the margins. The collaboration and collective power I experienced during these years showed me what was possible when communities, activists, scholars, and decision-makers came together to talk, strategize, dream, and realize a small part of a shared vision of humanity.

5

A Crisis of Demand

'Ours is not a caravan of despair.
Come, even if you have broken your vows a thousand times.
Come, yet again, come, come.'

—*Jalal al-din Rumi*

I was in awe standing in front of the bust of Nefertiti—an Egyptian queen in fourteenth century BC and one of the most famous and beautiful women of the ancient world. It was hard to believe that I was at the Neues Museum in East Berlin, a visit made possible for a small group of special guests invited by the German Government in 1991. It was a pivotal moment in history. The Berlin Wall had collapsed, marking the end of the Cold War and with it, the ideological divisions, proxy wars, and superpower rivalries. The small group were leaders of the Society for International Development, a network that promoted social justice and fostered democratic participation in development. Professor Richard Jolly was its vice president and chairman of its North/South Roundtable. The network attracted leading thinkers like Nobel Laureate Amartya Sen and Louis Emmerij, president of the OECD Development Centre and former Rector of the Institute of Social Studies. I was invited to some of their meetings, including the Berlin meeting, as I knew several key members from my academic and ILO days. After the museum visit, the bus tour took us past buildings still in ruins from the 1945 bombing raids on the Nazi capital during World War II. Louis Emmerij invited me for coffee to reflect deeper on what we had just experienced, and how the world came together to rise from the ashes of the war—the most destructive in recorded history.

We spoke of the birth of the United Nations and the UN Charter agreed to by all member states with the leadership of the United States as the best way to forge an inclusive rule-based multilateral world order for big and small nations, and for countries coming out of colonialism and searching for new pathways of development. It was a transformational moment. We discussed the powerful ideas and aspirations embedded in the UN Charter that starts with 'We the Peoples', as governments promised every individual, in every country, an equal claim to dignity, respect, and happiness based on freedom from want and freedom from fear as the foundation for sustaining a peaceful and prosperous world. However, we were both frustrated that there had not been enough practical changes on the ground and in our institutions, and the powerful norms remained unfulfilled promises.

As the Cold War era melted away with the fall of the Berlin Wall in 1989, the UN could once again wield the moral authority of its Charter to mobilize the idealism and collective power of nations to pursue a more inclusive global order for the twenty-first century based on the rules of multilateralism. The international cooperation and mutual trust that flowed from it could open up new possibilities and free the energies of countries to work together again for renewed economic and social progress in the globalizing world. Our Berlin meeting was a start to that global conversation.

It was a time of great promise. Governments gathered to address how to shape a fairer world founded on shared values and common responsibilities, to make life freer and peaceful. This was done through an unprecedented series of UN world conferences, starting with the World Summit on Children (1990), the Earth Summit (1992), the World Conference on Human Rights (1993), the International Conference on Population and Development (1994), the World Summit for Social Development (1995), and the FWCW (1995). These conferences provided the momentum for the world community—governments and civil society, men and women—to unite in solidarity to work for a holistic development paradigm that put people and the planet at the centre of decision-making. The dominant feeling was one of hope. Tens of thousands of women, from civil society as well as marginalized communities, participated actively in the UN conferences, mobilizing to establish new norms and agendas to dismantle entrenched discrimination and pursue more collective and sustainable economic and social freedom.

Encouraged by this new wave of optimism, the preparations for the FWCW were in full swing by 1993. I was excited to lead the Asia-Pacific NGO preparatory process for this conference that was to be held in Beijing, China. The UN conferences promised to deliver an inclusive agenda for change in an unequal world. For this to have real meaning, I wanted to ensure that the multilateral system gave voice to the realities, insights, and strategies of women frequently ignored by decision-makers and the multilateral system itself. It was an opportunity to strengthen social movements, women's civil society, and community groups to impact public policies, norms, and values using the UN platform. With resources from UNIFEM and various donor governments, I used my position at APDC and our networks to connect women from different parts of the region who were previously politically isolated from one another—women from the socialist countries of China, Mongolia, Vietnam, Laos, and

Cambodia with women from the Pacific islands, South Asia, East Asia and the Association of Southeast Asian Nations (ASEAN) countries. I consciously created spaces and occasions for women to engage with research teams and decision-makers beyond ideological divides so that there was mutual understanding of the social inequality and the diversity in our region. It was a unique moment for new conversations and understanding, to embrace women's insights and strategies.

Many women from the socialist countries were at the front lines of change. They had been struggling to remove existing legal and structural barriers faced by women in the economy and were keen to strengthen female labour force participation in higher wage and growth sectors as their countries undertook structural reforms with the collapse of the Soviet Union. I took the opportunity to organize a regional conference in Hanoi, Vietnam, to study two reports issued at that time and influenced development and public policies. The UNDP had published the first Human Development Report in 1990 by Pakistani economist Mahbub ul Haq and Amartya Sen. It provided an inspiring, theoretically grounded framework that focused on people and how development is more than just the gross national product (GNP) growth. The World Bank had started to go beyond its early structural adjustment approach to focus on poverty, growth, and economic restructuring in its 1990 World Development Report. But this was still within the framework associated with macroeconomic adjustments, and the UNDP report provided a fresh, convincing alternative. I brought academics and decision-makers to interact with women from the region, across ideology, to learn what works in different contexts, exchange good ideas and strategies, and inspire each other. This helped to build collaboration on shared ideas and shared agendas, to think big and improve gender equality as the foundation to support strong, inclusive growth and enhance the resilience and dynamism of societies.

A fertile ground had opened to build women's leadership from the ground up and unite new coalitions for social change that could shake the roots of despair and rejuvenate the spirit of hope in communities left behind. It was the opportunity to connect the aspirations of local people to global institutions and the international community. For this to be meaningful, I placed great importance on engaging with women in their communities to understand what is really going on, feel the pulse of specific local contexts, and hear the narratives on what needed to change. We travelled to meet with nomadic families tending their animals on the steppes of Mongolia to understand their experience of the major economic transition in the country with the collapse of the Soviet Union. We listened to the aspirations of women in Indo-China recalling their leadership in war and peace, the way they survived bombings and violence and were then determined to rebuild their countries and their lives. We learned from feminist leaders in India and Pakistan on how they were repairing people-to-people relationships, fostering peace after the trauma of the Partition. We worked with female Chinese farmers living through the break-up of the communal system and the shift to the household responsibility system and the market economy. We talked to women in urban slums and supported young women in the textile factories of Bangladesh to improve their working conditions. This inclusive engagement harnessed new energy and ideas from our different communities, capturing the deep chords of women's existence.

These voices and realities were captured in several APDC publications: *Daughters in Industry, Women Farmers, Missing Women, Market Growth and State Planning,* and resource books on *Women and the Environment, Women and Health, Women and Law.*

The publications were used to prepare for the FWCW and in the APDC policy dialogues to reveal the structures that have restricted women's lives, capture women's contribution, show how women were central to the region's economic and social progress, and recommend actions that would enable women to improve their quality of living. I believed that as the Asia-Pacific underwent rapid change and shattered ideological dichotomies, development could become a transformative practice, unleashing women's full potential and reshaping the future.

The extraordinary mobilization of women, across borders and continents, cultivated relationships and reservoirs of knowledge and laid the foundation for vibrant regional and global coalitions that revitalized common understanding and common directions based on shared values. We were able to nurture the Asia Pacific Forum on Women, Law and Development (APWLD) network and draw on the expertise of our member—Women Living under Muslim Law—to share their experiences and knowledge with partners in Malaysia and Indonesia at a time when Middle East politics was increasingly influencing the direction of Muslim societies in South East Asia. The network was a useful resource for Muslim women, exposing them to diverse interpretations of Islam as a counterbalance to the Saudi Arabian interpretation of Sunni and Wahabi Islam.

My APDC programme also became the regional platform for global networks and institutions to engage on issues ranging from economic globalization to media and communication. The global network of feminist economists—Development Alternatives with Women for a New Era (DAWN)—initiated by Indian economists Devaki Jain and Gita Sen, appointed me as its Southeast Asian coordinator to help articulate economics from the perspective of poor women and build a new paradigm where women shaped decisions for inclusive growth in a globalizing economy.

This level of mobilization and energy for a regional preparatory process of the UN, linking the local to the regional and the global, was unprecedented. Women genuinely had faith that these UN processes would deliver 'Equality, Development, and Peace'—the promise of the First World Conference on Women, which was held in 1975 in Mexico City.

ESCAP was in charge of regional preparations of UN global conferences and wanted to organize a small expert group meeting, as they have traditionally done according to UN bureaucratic rules. For me, if women had to change themselves and their world, then it was time to have a different discourse and hear the struggles and perspectives of women, including from the local communities, who had been silenced for long, and not just the experts and the articulated few. Furthermore, the UN opened a new opportunity to connect community conversations with global dialogues. It provided the platform for cooperation with governments and civil society, connecting with one another to find ways to move their societies towards 'equality, development and peace'. We, therefore, pushed for the first-ever women's civil society conference to replace the expert group so that more women could come together to reflect, share experiences, and create the possibility for change. ESCAP staff resisted, but the supportive executive secretary, Mr Rafeeuddin Ahmed, the longest serving Under-Secretary-General in the United Nations, gave us his blessings to organize the conference after we met with him. The process of mobilizing women to engage, shape their compelling narrative, and reimagine a world free from poverty, violence, and discrimination was perhaps the most important aspect of the Fourth World Conference on Women. This innovative approach allowed women to trust the UN as a space to articulate their vision and priorities for peace and security and economic and social development.

Leading and facilitating the civil society consultation process was not without serious tensions. It was an unprecedented encounter of diversity across the historical divisions of class, race, politics, and geography. Due to the vast diversity of women, there were competing agendas, strategies, and views based on political differences among women themselves. A small group of radical women wanted more political control over the process and outcomes of the conference. They thought that I was too moderate in my approach to seek a common ground and find ways to keep people together. I persisted and empowered various groups to champion their own issues and methods to hold powerful people and institutions accountable to the commitments made at the series of UN conferences. Difficult as they were, the negotiations that I facilitated resulted in the first civil society action agenda in the Asia-Pacific forged by over 1,000 women's groups and networks from the region which was not on 'women's issues', but on the renewal of our globalizing world 'through women's eyes'.

Preparations for the conference also allowed me the opportunity to be a bridge, helping China to better understand civil engagement and non-governmental organizations, over 30,000 of whom worldwide would be descending on China for the conference. I remembered a senior Chinese official at one of the meetings whispered anxiously to me in private: 'If they are non-governmental, what are they?' I had to explain they were citizens' groups with diverse interests, views, and expectations, and that the UN global conferences provided the platform for women's civil society to engage with governments, striving together to narrow development gaps for greater equality.

A few months later, after the successful Asia-Pacific consultation, I was appointed the Executive Director of UNIFEM. My appointment marked a milestone for me as well as the organization, as I was their first Executive Director to be appointed from outside North America. It was not an easy choice for me to return to the UN and be based alone in New York with my daughters. I remembered my earlier ESCAP experience, but realized from the preparatory process for the FWCW that the UN had the global legitimacy to convene governments at the highest level to establish norms and standards and the authority to advance women's empowerment and protect women's human rights everywhere. Also, many enlightened people had joined or rejoined the UN to provide leadership to manage the institution and guide the multilateral journey in the era of globalization. They saw new possibilities for greater peace with justice and development based not on ideology, but on the values of the UN Charter to shape a shared destiny 'free from want, free from fear'. It was hard not to be inspired and rise to the challenge.

There were personal reasons, too, that urged me to accept the job offer. The world of opposition politics was cruel to families and to relationships. Yew Teng's focus was always on a higher plane of principles, not on building a career in the type of politics that was practised. He took to politics to change his world and could not stand the compromises he witnessed and started to tear them down unforgivingly. To survive on my one-year contract and protect my children from the resulting nastiness of politics that surrounded him, I learned to create a two-track world. He had his world that I refused to be pulled into, and I had my professional world that he respected and did not participate in. What kept us together was our deep love for our children and for one another. The home I created was to be a sanctuary that would keep our worldly engagements outside. It did not fully work out and tensions grew so that my leaving for New York with the children provided some distance that we both needed. However, our daughters and I made it a point to call Yew Teng every weekend and return to visit him as often as we could.

The deep love that the children and I had for Yew Teng survived the upheavals of politics to renew itself through generously giving each other space to breathe and by coming together regularly.

I had been headhunted for several jobs at the UN and the World Bank before the UNIFEM offer, but the timing would never be right. I wanted the children to grow up with their father and our extended family, so I found ways to be self-empowered and effective in my work at APDC. At the same time, I knew that the future of APDC was dependent on its leadership and the nature of its governing board, which had started to select people who were less innovative and more conservative. It was, therefore, better for me to leave at the height of my career there, when I was still highly appreciated and given the authority to select my successor. I selected Vanessa Griffen, a feminist academic from Fiji who worked very closely with me and in the women's movement in the Pacific.

Saving UNIFEM

A thunderous applause rang through the UN conference hall in Vienna on 15 October 1994. The European Preparatory Meeting for the FWCW was taking place at the Vienna International Centre, and I had just presented my new directions for UNIFEM to the plenary and major donors as its new Executive Director. The meeting was chaired by Patricia Licuanan from our Philippines migration network, who was then the chairperson of the UN Commission on the Status of Women—the intergovernmental structure in charge of the global preparations for the FWCW.

When my appointment was first announced, Bella Abzug, an iconic feminist leader and member of the US House of Representatives wrote in the *Earth Times* that it was celebrated by the global women's movement. Later, in Washington, Joan Dunlop, founder and president of the International Women's Health Coalition, invited me to address a major international conference. She said in her introduction that if there was a global women's vote for the position, I would win outright. The endorsement of my appointment as the first Executive Director from outside North America by these influential leaders gave me courage, but could not prepare me for the institutional storms and bureaucratic battles ahead—the financial crisis in UNIFEM, politics of mainstreaming, and structural position of UNIFEM within the UN.

On arrival in New York, on 25 October, I quickly settled into my position, facilitated by my long relationship with UNIFEM from the time of both its first and second directors—Margaret Snyder and Sharon Capeling-Alakija. During the first month in office, the deputy director informed me that there was a temporary cash flow problem of $1.1 million due to delays in payment of government contributions. She assured me that this was quite normal in the UN. However, before the holiday season, on 22 December 1994, UNIFEM's chief of management services worriedly presented me with a financial statement prepared by the UNDP Division of Finance. It stated that UNIFEM recorded 'a deficit of $6,804,811 for the period ending 30 September 1994' with an expected deficit of $9.8 million by the end of 1994. Not to disrupt the holidays, I waited till 3 January 1995 to inform the former executive director, Sharon Capeling-Alakija, of my concern and ask her advice on the matter, given that the core contribution from governments at that time was about $9 million annually. She was concerned and said she would send a financial team from UNDP to advise what could be done. The situation worsened by 6 January when I was presented with another statement indicating that UNIFEM recorded a deficit of $13.21 million at the end of 1994. This time I feared we had a serious financial problem and decided to take matters into my own hands. I informed the administrator of UNDP, James Gustave Speth, and requested a financial audit of UNIFEM.

The audit detailed the nature of the crisis and raised the level of the deficit to $13.6 million. The report provided a technical analysis of the problem, stating that since 1991, UNIFEM had been under pressure to reduce its unspent resources, and over-allocation to spend was allowed under the 'the partial funding formula'. UNIFEM had over-programmed over a protracted period based on delays in financial information, inaccurate interpretation of its expenditure, and financial position. As budget revisions were not done in a timely manner, there was the reallocation of obligated but unused resources. While appreciating these technical concerns that could be fixed, for me, the real problem was an underfunded women's fund in the UN. The preparations for the FWCW stretched the fund and exacerbated the situation, as women's groups funded by UNIFEM increased their activities and spending. It was as though they all cashed their chips simultaneously. But, government contributions to UNIFEM had fallen way behind.

It was a dangerous time for the organization to be in a bad financial situation. The UN reform was high on the agenda with ongoing efforts to merge small entities. Besides UNIFEM, the interlocking structure for work on women in the UN included two other organizations. The Division for the Advancement of Women (DAW) in the UN Secretariat was the body that convened UN meetings and intergovernmental negotiations, so they were the formal secretariat for the women's conferences. The International Research and Training Institute for the Advancement of Women (INSTRAW) was a small research and training institute, based in Santo Domingo, and was intended to generate and harmonize all of the UN's work on research and training on the advancement of women. It was struggling to survive. Already in 1993, there was a serious attempt to merge INSTRAW with UNIFEM that failed because of a strong objection from the Government of the Dominican Republic, the host country of INSTRAW, as a large number of their local staff would be displaced if it was relocated to New York.

It was a highly complex and politicized environment to navigate, as major donors regarded gender mainstreaming to be the necessary strategy for the advancement of women. They had, therefore, supported gender units and focal points of large agencies and allocated more resources to strengthen their capacity to influence the work and decision-making of their organizations. With declining support for separate entities working on issues affecting women, UNIFEM, as an autonomous fund in close association with UNDP, had to constantly justify its existence and impact to donors. There was already a White Paper on UN Reform endorsed by the United States government that recommended the absorption of UNIFEM into UNDP. The executive board of UNDP, to which UNIFEM reported, had donors who supported that position. As a governing body, they were already angry about the financial problem.

The chair of the UNIFEM Consultative Committee— another governance layer of one member state from each of the five UN regions—invited me to lunch. She was from Austria representing the donor group and wanted to discuss the situation. As the chair, she expressed deep concern over the complexity of the problems facing UNIFEM as well as the serious turf wars, intense competition over resources, and political intrigues within the system which she thought I was too inexperienced, as an outsider, to fully understand and manage. I responded that I had no interest in intrigues, that I was committed to the organization.

I would engage with the issues and operate from a position of courage and strength, not from fear and weakness.

My priority was to demonstrate that I was a determined leader in full charge during this turbulence. There was the urgent need to keep staff morale high while I addressed the financial difficulties, the downsizing and reorganization of UNIFEM. I called a staff meeting to say that I refused to accept the mainstream narrative in the manner it was cast. I had already written officially to the administrator of UNDP on 9 January to say, 'The problem that faces us is not a crisis of existence. If anything, it indicates a crisis of demand.' I felt that the UN should be embarrassed to have such a small development fund for women that it had gone into deficit supporting women organizing for the FWCW. Of course there was the need for a better financial management system and responsibility, but most important for a financially stronger UNIFEM. Soon after, I addressed the angry executive board to get its support by saying, 'There is a point beyond anger. You are angry but so am I. I came to lead UNIFEM into the FWCW, not to solve a financial crisis. But UNIFEM is an institution worth saving because it is the main UN fund that supports women in the developing world. There are three questions: Do I know the problem? Do I know the solution? Am I the right person? My answer is yes to the first two, but I need your support for the third.' With UNIFEM's allies in the board, the governing body eventually gave me three years to address the deficit and bring the budget to zero balance.

It was a humiliating experience for the organization, as it had to put its internal systems in order and deal with its funding crisis. I immediately established a financial crisis taskforce to supervise budget cuts, rephrase projects, non-renewal of short-term contracts (which the majority of the staff were on), and freeze half of our core posts. I had to work closely with the UNDP's Division of Finance to design a budget strategy and meet monthly with Associate Administrator Rafeeuddin Ahmed, the former executive secretary of ESCAP, who was sympathetic throughout.

We were cut to the bones on the eve of the FWCW. I was called in alone for an urgent meeting with the Gus Speth and his senior managers to discuss the existential pressures and the future of UNIFEM. The proposal before me was to accept the offer of $10 million a year from UNDP for the programmes of UNIFEM and in return to give up its autonomy and be integrated fully with UNDP as part of the gender mainstreaming agenda. They all saw resource mobilization and UNIFEM's future as too difficult to manage in an increasingly hostile environment to small entities in the United Nations. I rejected the proposal immediately and said, 'What do I say to the women of the developing world whom UNIFEM had supported? That I came to the UN from the developing world on the eve of the FWCW, to close its Women's Fund? Thank you for the offer of the $10 million but I will raise it myself. Give me two years, the term of my contract, to strengthen UNIFEM and if I fail I will tell our women's constituency myself. Till then, UNIFEM will remain an autonomous Fund.'

Downhearted, I went back to organize my regular staff meeting to alert them of the strong external forces waiting to define the nature of our existence. I stressed the urgency of action to be in charge of our own future and demonstrate our capacity and impact. We did not have three years to address the deficit. We needed to do it immediately. I needed high-level commitment from outside the UN to help us steer through the storm. I shared my decision to visit donor capitals to engage with the highest level of decision-makers and our constituencies with a totally different strategy—a new way of presenting the narrative of mainstreaming to build an effective coalition of support. I made the argument that the FWCW provided us the biggest opportunity to embrace change, rethink our position in the UN, and reshape the ways we engage. We needed to be at the forefront of intergovernmental discourse shaping the understanding of gender mainstreaming, to be the most strategic UN organization, leading the way in women's empowerment and gender equality, innovative thinking, as well as mobilization on the ground to transform the mainstream.

My vision was to reposition UNIFEM as the indispensable vehicle and knowledge leader in the UN, the heart for the implementation of the women's empowerment agenda coming out of the FWCW. This demanded a dramatic shift and transformation of our traditional role, which was to provide small grants to women on the ground. It was no longer enough; our constituency had grown. These women's groups could be funded directly and UNIFEM should not be competing with them for donor funding. To be relevant, we needed to embrace our UN identity and establish UNIFEM as the UN organization with the best knowledge, partnerships, and experience on how to mobilize and empower women to realize their potential and cocreate fairer societies in the mainstream. UNIFEM had to show its capacity to galvanize global leadership and that it had the networks to engage with the span and diversity of different geographical regions, opening doors for female leaders and organizations. To be of value, we had to show that we knew not just how to strengthen women's mobilization but also to promote strong collaboration between the women's movement and the UN as a system and its member states to implement the commitments from all the various UN conferences.

My experience in working on the international migration of domestic workers in Asia gave me the confidence that we could forge alliances and agreements that would be equally beneficial in the transformation of women's lives and that of our countries as they work for economic, social, and environmentally sustainable development. In other words, UNIFEM could be the beacon for mainstreaming the agenda and investing in women's agency to move critical issues from the periphery to the centre of decision-making, and, in the process, help our countries navigate the complexities of the globalizing world, transforming development and accelerating change to a more inclusive and fairer world.

Turning the Tide

In preparation for my numerous visits to address donors in their capitals, I worked hard writing the guiding vision for the organization, entitled 'A Women's Development Agenda for the 21st Century'. It linked analysis with practice for the type of changes we would like to see in the twenty-first century—women's economic empowerment in the globalizing economy, women's political empowerment for accountable governance, realizing women's human rights and ending VAW, and women's role in sustaining peace. I mobilized support from the best academic thinkers, activists, and political leaders I knew—from Amartya Sen, Nafis Sadik, Ellen Johnson Sirleaf, Lourdes Arizpe to Charlotte Bunch, Juan Somavia, Gita Sen and so many others. Since my time as an academic at IDS, I had kept my links with global research institutes and networks of people who were drivers of change in thinking and action, building new approaches to economic and social development. The gender and development programmes of APDC and UNIFEM both had historical roots that went back to the UN First World Conference on Women and I quickly became a part of global feminist networks. These webs of relationships became my ecosystem of support. Every person I approached responded positively and produced quality material in record time. They helped to synthesize the critical issues and key recommendations from the various UN conferences on women's empowerment—how to energize governments to implement them and how to translate the recommendations into innovative and catalytic programmes for UNIFEM's support.

Their contributions were put together in an edited volume, entitled *A Commitment to the World's Women*, our flagship publication for the transformation to a more equal world, launched at the FWCW. It was a bestseller for several months at Women's Ink of the International Women's Tribune Centre, an information and communication coalition distributing analyses and perspectives of women from the Global South. It was eventually sold out at the FWCW in Beijing. In retrospect, I believe that our engagement with some of the world's top thinkers and leaders to provide solid analysis, strategy, and practical recommendations helped to win back the trust of donors and member states. We showed that UNIFEM had the capacity to envision, galvanize support at multiple levels, and deliver on a transformative agenda for women and development.

The Netherlands was the first that came to UNIFEM's rescue when I visited donor capitals to articulate my vision and strategy for UNIFEM and win their confidence, supported by a network of feminist leaders. The Minister of Development Corporation, Jan Pronk, wrote me the nicest letter, dated 13 July 1995, saying, 'I have taken note of the optimism and confidence with which you are facing the future, specifically after the FWCW in Beijing. I think UNIFEM in its present situation needs a Director like you, with vision, drive and the ability to see the opportunities ahead.' He gave us a one-time contribution of $3 million to address the deficit with an increase in the annual contribution. I also managed to secure increased contributions from several other core donors with my promise of developing a business plan to deliver on the outcomes of the FWCW. We worked with US women's groups and our National Committee to prevent proposed budget cuts in US contribution.

The tide was turning. In early May 1995, the ADB invited me to address a meeting of its board of governors in Auckland, which allowed me to not just prevent a budget cut from the Government of New Zealand, but also to get a tripling of their contribution. I presented not just my agenda for the FWCW, but also mapped out my implementation strategy in the context of the UN reforms to the Ministry of Foreign Affairs—the Department in charge of New Zealand's Official Development Aid—and Members of Parliament, many of whom I knew from my days as a student leader and through my work in the Pacific while at APDC. They were convinced that I knew how to work the system and deliver. It helped that I was invited to address the highest body of the ADB. I worked hard to diversify and widen our resource base, and succeeded in building strong relationships with many developing countries from the Group of 77 that contributed for the first time, led by its chair, the Government of the Philippines, which increased its funding by 100 per cent on the basis of my previous relationship and work on the international migration of domestic workers. In addition, UNIFEM staff obtained funding from the governments of Japan, Sweden, and Switzerland, and the MacArthur Foundation, to work towards the FWCW. Also, to help manage the deficit, Mr Speth absolved the $4 million missing advances to UNIFEM due to the inability to track the Inter-Office Vouchers used before the digital age. All this meant that our potential deficit was reduced significantly to $4.5 million by the middle of 1995, before the conference. With the support of so many, I felt a deep sense of international solidarity.

Despite this turnaround, not everyone in UNIFEM agreed with my new direction for the long term. Some staff even suggested that the crisis was a ploy by UNDP to absorb us, which I dismissed. The head of the Latin-American Division, Ana Maria, whom I highly respected, warned that I was making a terrible mistake by focusing on the UN, as it was too bureaucratic, not a friendly system for women, and would be very hard to change. There was also too much tension between the DAW in the Secretariat and UNIFEM ever since our first director shifted the fund from the Secretariat to UNDP. At the end she said, despite the disruption, there would be nothing to show during my term. She wanted to protect me from failure and reminded me of what my predecessors did: Margaret Snyder concentrated on putting money directly in the hands of women to support their projects and Sharon Capeling-Alakija provided small grants to support women's civil society organizing for the UN conferences. I shared how my work at APDC benefited from the steadfast support of both directors, whom I respected greatly, and how we had to continue to build on their solid foundations and strong support for local women and women's organizing. But the times were changing, bringing new challenges and new opportunities, including for the UN itself. I felt that we must read the signs, help build the UN we want, and find the courage to transform and reposition UNIFEM to think big and bring about stronger policies and government actions for women in the changing world—or we could lose the organization.

My secretary, Esther, must have overheard this conversation, as she came up to me later and said, 'Do you hear how people in the UN greet each other while waiting for the lifts? When asked "how are you", the answer is "surviving". People have learned to just survive in this system. By bringing about change you are disrupting the space they have created for survival. Change is difficult. People in the UN system work in packs. You are alone.' I responded that the lift we were in was in a shaky structure. We had been internally weakened and compelled to shift position, not just to survive, but to thrive. Although I put up a brave face, this encounter disturbed me and underpinned the difficulties of overcoming entrenched interest, deeply embedded behavioural norms, and changing organizational culture in a huge bureaucracy.

I spent that night in deep thought, feeling very alone. Around 8 p.m., there was a knock at my office door. It was Joanne Sandler, a part-time consultant working with the publications and communications section of UNIFEM. Joanne asked how I was. I replied that the struggle was very hard, and the staff divided. We had been so distracted and weakened by the financial crisis when we should be united and totally engaged with the FWCW, providing directions and substance and positioning UNIFEM for the implementation of the Platform for Action coming out of the conference in Beijing. UNIFEM had to emerge quickly from its financial problem that had absorbed our energy and created so much uncertainty and insecurity among the staff. I told her that I was putting together a resource mobilization and constituency-building strategy as well as a whole new approach to the way we would be performing in Beijing. I said, 'We will not go wearing sackcloth and ashes; we are small but we will play it big. However, to succeed in the hostile external environment and in the context of UN reform, UNIFEM will need a guardian angel'. Early the next morning, there was another knock at my door. When I opened it, there was Joanne wearing a pair of angel wings, chiming: 'Reporting for duty!'

Joanne gave me new energy and new hope. She brought back my smile and laughter. She had already told me that she did not believe in institutions but was committed as a consultant to UNIFEM. I said that I needed her full commitment to help rebuild UNIFEM. There was no need for many words between us. I just asked: 'One year?' There were no resources in UNIFEM for any position, as we were financially depleted. I went straight to

Mr. Speth to request help, saying that I needed a one-year position fully funded to help UNIFEM prepare for the FWCW and its implementation. The administrator of UNDP was sympathetic and I had the one-year position. Joanne made a big difference to the organization. She helped me manage the change process, and in a difficult external environment became my 'resonance chamber' and most trusted colleague. She was creative and a superb facilitator for many of our strategy-planning meetings as we started our preparations turning the Fourth World Conference on Women into the Women's Conference on the State of the World, and its renewal for the twenty-first century through women's eyes.

Reimagining the World through Women's Eyes

The 1995 FWCW was perhaps the largest world conference ever held by the United Nations till that time. The participation was huge: Over 30,000 women participated in the NGO forum held in Huairou from 30 August to 8 September, and 17,000 people mainly from governments registered for the official UN conference held in Beijing from 4 to 15 September. At the opening ceremony, I carried the UNIFEM Peace Torch with African leaders across the National Olympic Stadium and passed it from hand to hand, lighting up the conference as 30,000 women cheered, cried and sang the anthem, 'Keep on Moving Forward'.

The idea of the peace torch came from the African team of UNIFEM, especially Laketch Dirasse who was in charge of our African Women in Crisis Countries (AFWIC) programme, when we discussed how to ensure the dynamism, highest visibility, and impact of UNIFEM at the lowest cost during the FWCW. I went a step further to suggest that we light the flame in South Africa which gained independence from apartheid in 1994, becoming the most inspiring country in the twentieth century, as President

Nelson Mandela triumphed over hatred and united the nation for peace and renewal. We lit the peace flame of renewal with Frene Ginwala, the Speaker of the National Assembly of South Africa, at sunrise in KwaZulu-Natal, the place that recovered from some of the worst violence. From South Africa, the torch travelled to several war-torn countries where UNIFEM supported women's peacemaking. The peace torch was received by the leaders and youth of the conflict-affected countries before reaching Beijing to light the flame of inspiration for the FWCW. Although we were not allowed to tell the story of the peace torch because of what some staff believed to be organizational rivalry from the Secretariat annoyed at our visibility, UNIFEM was covered on the front pages of the *New York Times*, *China Daily*, and several other newspapers around the world.

The theme of the conference was 'Equality, Development, and Peace'. For women, equality, development, and peace are inextricably intertwined. What women wanted was nothing less than the transformation of the twenty-first century to ensure that our daughters had the same opportunities as our sons, where women could realize their rights to quality education, employment, and healthcare; equal inheritance, legal protection, and citizenship; and be free from violent conflicts, harassment, and sexual violence. Women knew that they must be the primary agents of this transformation. Hence, the outcome that they sought from the FWCW was a global commitment for the empowerment of all women. And women's global activism was at its height, forming connections across deep divides to shape this global agenda.

It was time to bridge the local and the global, going beyond inter-state cooperation to forge collaborative relationships with women's organizations to achieve common goals. UNIFEM staff were energized and played lead roles as speakers and moderators at various panel discussions during the FWCW, focusing on women's economic and political empowerment to reimagine our world and remake societies where all women and girls could flourish, leading empowered lives in healthy communities and workplaces. I supervised over thirty UNIFEM events with my team along the following three themes: globalization and women's economic empowerment, women's leadership and political empowerment, and women's human rights and ending VAW. Throughout the conference, UNIFEM galvanized the participation of female leaders from civil society and local communities around the world, initiating dialogues between NGOs and government delegations over gains made during previous UN conferences so as not to lose ground during intergovernmental negotiations.

We had invited United States First Lady Hillary Rodham Clinton; Muhammad Yunus, the managing director of the Grameen Bank in Bangladesh; Ela Bhatt, the founder and general secretary of the Self-Employed Women's Association in India; and Esther Ocloo, the chairperson of the Sustainable End of Hunger Foundation in Ghana. I moderated the panel they were on to a packed house. Together, they created a lot of excitement, focusing on 'banking on the poor' and launching the global microfinance agenda to remove the financial constraints faced by women in the informal sector. This event was part of our theme on globalization and economic restructuring. My staff also organized a pavilion that emphasized the importance of science and technology, and several panels on women's economic security and rights and empowering women in the changing world of work. It was also an opportunity to advance social labelling to improve the working conditions of women in the factories of global supply chains, using the pressure from the growing ethical consumer market of middle-class women with purchasing power.

The second theme, on political empowerment, opened up innovative ways of building alliance, connecting, and communicating, and diving deep into the issues of power and leadership. Our small, but highly motivated team, worked closely with our networks to organize high-level roundtables on governance, leadership, and decision-making, and also women's leadership in reconciliation and peace. The panel on women and politics involved female political leaders and strengthened the dialogue and collaboration among ministers, parliamentarians, local government, and civil society. The third theme was building on the gains of previous UN conferences. It was organized in partnership with feminist leaders around the world. This included panels on ending violence against women, strengthening the Convention on the Elimination of All Forms of Discrimination against Women (CEDAW), cosponsoring the Global Tribunal on Accountability for Women's Human Rights, and investing in youth, entitled 'Today's Girls—Tomorrow's Women' which was organized together with indigenous leader and Nobel Laureate Rigoberta Menchu from Guatemala. In addition to participating in all these activities, I was the keynote speaker or panelist in over twenty other events organized by various women's groups, governments, and other UN agencies. UNIFEM was everywhere—engaging with new ideas, discussing new possibilities.

The finale celebrated UNIFEM's twentieth anniversary— 'Twenty Years of Commitment to the World's Women'—at the Beijing Royal International Club, made possible by private sector funding and the creative work of UNIFEM staff. It was a magical night with actress Jane Fonda hosting the event in the presence of over 1,000 senior leaders from government, civil society, the UN, and the local business community. Princess Basma Bint Talal, of Jordan—the Goodwill Ambassador of UNIFEM—UNDP Administrator Gus Speth, and I addressed the occasion. Together

with distinguished women leaders, we presented the UNIFEM
Anniversary awards to governments, organizations, and individuals
who had demonstrated extraordinary commitment to the world's
women. They included the Government of the Netherlands for
its outstanding commitment to the advancement of women in
developing countries, and honouring Jan Pronk, as the Minister
for Development Co-operation. We honoured the Government
of Sweden for its fully gender-balanced cabinet in 1995 and the
Government of South Africa for the way it struggled against
apartheid and worked to increase gender-sensitivity in governance.
We celebrated individual leaders like Helvi Sipila, the first woman
to hold the position of UN assistant secretary general and used
it to organize the First World Conference on Women in 1975.
We also honoured Graca Machel and the African Women's Peace
Network for building strong coalitions for reconciliation and
peace. It was a wonderful way to inspire and motivate, and to
honour the power of our networks and our champions.

We had indeed ensured the dynamism, highest visibility, and
impact of UNIFEM at the lowest cost during the FWCW while
helping governments and the UN Secretariat with the difficult
negotiation sessions during the conference. All this contributed
very substantively to the Beijing Platform for Action (BPA)
and its twelve critical areas of concern—the intergovernmental
framework from the FWCW—finally becoming the agenda
for women's empowerment. The critical areas of the concerns
identified were women and poverty, education and training of
women, women and health, VAW, women and armed conflict,
women and the economy, women in power and decision-making,
mechanisms for the advancement of women, human rights of
women, women and the media, women and the environment,
and the girl child. This became the steering document for the
UN and its member states to forge a civilized world in which

social arrangements, laws, institutions, and practices no longer discriminate against women and there are equal opportunities and pathways of larger freedom and dignity for women and girls. I felt that we had transformed UNIFEM's crisis into an opportunity, and that my team had regained its strength and confidence, fully charged to take up the post-Beijing agenda.

UNIFEM: Innovator and Catalyst for Change

As I addressed the FWCW and listened to governments and UN leaders rallying behind UNIFEM, I felt a sense of relief that our work had paid off. UNDP Administrator Gus Speth called for our resources to 'double and double again'. At one lunch meeting, he passed a handwritten message to me that said that, dollar for dollar, I had the highest impact and visibility in the United Nations Development Group. At the Pledging Conference after the FWCW, many countries increased their contribution by over 100 per cent, most by 30 to 100 per cent, and several developing countries contributed for the first time. Our core resources grew by almost 60 per cent, and we got out of our financial crisis in the record time of a year, with the UNDP Executive Board approving a budget of $6 million to be 'strategically invested'. A Dutch official said to one of my staff members that UNIFEM had become 'a blue chip' worthy of larger investment. I knew that this was because of the deep emotional commitment of my staff to work against the grain to make an impact on women's lives.

With the increased trust and resources provided, pressure was on me and my team to demonstrate how we were going to deliver our new direction—our promise of UNIFEM being an innovator and a catalyst moving the mainstream to transform the lives of women by implementing the BPA. I immediately focused on two areas—first, to identify the strategic niche of UNIFEM to help harness the full potential of the UN to deliver for women in the changing landscape of challenges and opportunities; and second, to address the internal needs of the organization to enable UNIFEM to perform effectively in its niche of comparative advantage. I shifted UNIFEM from being a broad-based 'grant–awarding' organization for women to being a strategic fund, as well as an advocacy and learning organization within the UN system with experience in strengthening women's mobilization and alliance-building. Using the empowerment framework of the FWCW, my directors and I filtered all new proposals, accepting and funding those that contributed to policy or legal changes leading to women's economic and political empowerment, or those that piloted innovative approaches for women's empowerment and financing of gender equality which could be replicated on a wider scale.

At the same time, I took full advantage of the ongoing UN reform. My team and I built a niche for UNIFEM as a relevant player and catalytic resource in the new structures established within the UN system to implement the global consensus that emerged out of the major UN conferences. In particular, I acted as Chair for the Inter-Agency Operational Working Group on the Implementation of the Beijing Platform for Action, in close collaboration with Rosario Green, the newly established high-level gender adviser in the Secretary General's office. I also cooperated with DAW as secretariat for the Commission on the Status of Women, mandated by the UN General Assembly to be responsible for the follow-up process to implement the BPA.

A critical area that emerged as priority for action at FWCW was ending VAW. I successfully mobilized funding from the Government of Japan and worked with the General Assembly to establish the UN Trust Fund to End All Forms of Violence against Women, bringing together all parts of the UN system working on VAW. Another priority was the revitalization of the CEDAW. At the FWCW, the CEDAW committee had requested UNIFEM to be to CEDAW what UNICEF was to the Convention on the Rights of the Child (CRC). UNICEF was the powerful engine in the UN to help countries advance the implementation of their obligations when they had ratified or acceded to the CRC. This had helped transform children's lives in many parts of the world. Both CRC and CEDAW had the same status of international law requiring national action to put them into practice and submit regular national reports. However, the CEDAW committee members made up of independent experts, responsible for supervising the implementation of the convention, expressed deep disappointment that the international bill of rights for women had no such supportive arrangement. Hence, my staff, particularly Ilana Lewis and Lee Waldorf, who were in charge of UNIFEM's programme on CEDAW and women's human rights, worked closely with UNICEF to synthesize CEDAW and CRC to bring about a more effective implementation of common goals. With support from the Canadian Government, they also worked with the CEDAW committee to introduce CEDAW alternative reports that gave voice and legitimacy to women's groups in holding their governments accountable to the promises made. This was an innovation. UNIFEM used our resources to train women's groups in preparing and presenting these reports, as well as facilitating their engagement with CEDAW members and member states to follow up on its recommendations.

While dealing with the UN processes and governance in New York, my heart was with the women whom I had consulted with at the country and community levels during the preparatory process for the FWCW. This was where real change could have happened if we could have harnessed the full potential of the UN system on the ground. This required new ways of leading and learning in order to build trust and break through gridlocks and 'turf wars'.

I, therefore, worked to strengthen UNIFEM as an experienced advocate and knowledge provider at country and community levels, a valued resource for the Resident Coordinator (RC) system, newly established under UN reform. By using my country visits to forge a closer working relationship between UNIFEM regional programme advisers and the RCs, we made the implementation of the BFA an integral part of the United Nations Development Assistance Framework (UNDAF) and country strategies. The implementation and review of these strategies were not dependent on UNIFEM. Instead, it required building a unified alliance of the different UN agencies working at the country level to devise the coherent strategies.

As we grew in our resource base, I began to establish regional offices to replace single UNIFEM regional advisers and recruit quality teams of highly committed and skilled women, many of whom came from the women's movement and top universities and think tanks. Many had provided leadership during the various UN conferences and were substantively and politically strong. I wanted to make sure that the UN now had experienced professionals who knew how to build alliances with governments and local women, supporting and empowering them to participate meaningfully in the implementation of recommendations from the UN conferences and turning government commitments into real possibilities for progress. This was a very difficult process, as UNIFEM was administered by UNDP which had frozen external recruitment while it went through reforms and downsizing. I was asked to recruit from the list of 'floaters'. This I fully rejected, as it was the wrong fit and I was very clear about the type of team leadership and organizational capacities that I wanted to develop.

After hard negotiations, Debbie Landy, Director of UNDP's human resources, agreed to an arrangement that worked for all parties. We established specialized positions with contracts limited to UNIFEM. This arrangement allowed me to recruit excellent women and men, and gave me the freedom to recruit a dynamic team at the headquarters and in the regions. It also made it possible to attract top professionals like Diane Elson, who led the first Progress of the World's Women—an annual assessment that I had established. Together, we functioned as a community of purpose, guided by a common vision and direction, to refocus the organization on four areas: economic security and rights; building women's political leadership; realizing women's human rights with emphasis on ending violence against women; and women, peace, and security. The UNIFEM staff gave their best beyond the call of duty, playing increasingly prominent roles on the world stage in these areas. Mark Malloch Brown, the new Administrator of UNDP, remarked during his first visit that UNIFEM 'punched way above its weight' and we were 'too innovative to be a typical UN agency'. There was new energy in the organization.

While we were at the height of our achievement in 1998, little did we know that another crisis lay in wait. One day, at the crack of dawn, I received an urgent phone call from the UN security. In a panicked voice, the officer told me that the UNIFEM office had caught fire. I rushed to the office in disbelief. The entire floor was covered in black soot and everything was wet from the sprinklers. I later learned that one of my staff members had stayed late in the office to work. She had lit a scented candle near her computer and forgot to blow it off when leaving. Her room had caught fire. The flames spread quickly and engulfed the whole office. She was in shock, and so was all my staff. I knew I had to immediately calm everyone down and find a way to turn the situation around.

I told my staff that from the day I first arrived, I wondered why UNIFEM was stuck at the corner of the sixth floor of the FF building along East 45th Street. It was clearly time for us to obtain a better, friendlier office to work and interact. I had always wanted to create a work environment where there was a balance between work effectiveness and caring, where there was innovation and creativity with acceptance of mistakes. I had waited long enough for such a nurturing space where we could properly bond as motivated, creative, and committed people working towards common goals. That time had arrived.

There was a lovely office on the fifteenth floor of the FF building that had just been vacated by a private sector company. The timing could not have been better. Through skillful negotiation with the landlord and UNDP, we acquired it at a multi-year rent we could afford and soon shifted to the beautiful office with a balcony where we could see the East River. I had seized the crisis of fire and transformed it into an opportunity. It allowed us to move to a different space, leave behind the past, and build a new environment of strength for my staff. The new office on the 15th floor allowed UNIFEM the space to soar as an organization. UNIFEM had emerged from a major 'crisis of existence' with new resilience, vision, and hope. From the uncertainties of previous years, UNIFEM had grown in effectiveness and professionalism into a much needed and respected organization that delivered concrete results, with a fairly robust resource base supported by a plethora of new relationships and funding. It was time to celebrate our achievement and be a vehicle for women and social change.

As we navigated the institution safely through the storms, there were growing demands on us. I continued to emphasize the resource mobilization and constituency-building efforts of UNIFEM with full support from Joanne Sandler, while maintaining our low-cost culture through strategic partnerships. Together with the UNIFEM team, we inspired faith and commitment from both donor and programme countries, and from our women's constituency leading to significantly increased and diversified funding to UNIFEM. We were supported in a political environment where there were four powerful and sympathetic female ministers of International Development Cooperation—Claire Short from the United Kingdom, Eveline Herfkens from the Netherlands, Hilde Johnson from Norway, and Heidemarie Wieczorek-Zeul from Germany. By the end of 1998, as a result of substantive dialogue and consultation, the Department for International Development (DFID) of the United Kingdom increased its support by 237 per cent and produced an Institutional Strategy Paper that proposed a further contribution of $6 million. Norway increased its support by 45 per cent and South Africa by 100 per cent. We also secured $5.3 million from the UN Foundation, established by Ted Turner. Funding to the UN Trust Fund to End Violence against Women increased by 171 per cent. This funding trend continued, based on the result-oriented and high performance of the coherent team at UNIFEM with a strong sense of corporate identity and a firm grasp of the 'big picture'.

I succeeded in promoting Joanne to be the Deputy Executive Director of UNIFEM, the first without a UNDP contract. We worked closely together for ten years and grew the organization from a presence in twenty countries to a presence in 80 countries. By 2007, just before I was appointed United Nations Under-Secretary-General to head ESCAP, UNIFEM's annual core and non-core resources were about $150 million, used mainly to support programmes on women's economic security and rights; ending VAW; gender and HIV/AIDs; and women, peace, and security. We had unleashed our individual and organizational potential, harnessing our power to take on difficult issues, building movements and alliances to cocreate societies that treasured the dignity of women, and, in the words of Ralph Bunche when drafting the UN Charter, 'make change—even radical change—possible without violent upheaval'.

6

Breaking Silence and Shame

'We must not bend under the weight of spurious arguments invoking culture or traditional values. No value worth the name supports the oppression and enslavement of women . . . We will not allow ourselves to be silenced.'

—Nafis Sadik

A few months after the FWCW, I was invited on an official visit to Pakistan. As I entered the presidential palace, the voices of qawwali masters filled the air, rising like birds in flight as they offered their melodies of praise to the Beloved. It was easy to forget all the pain in the world on a night of such beauty. But I was in Pakistan to address the issue of VAW. As a guest of the President, General Pervez Musharraf, I was on a visit to develop cooperation with the Pakistani government and help the Ministry of Women's Affairs draft a strategic plan to implement the outcomes of the FWCW.

After the sublime musical performance, the President's wife asked me to share with her my impressions of my visit. I described my conversations with some of the women I had just met in a shelter supported by the Women's Ministry and with civil society groups. I told Mrs Musharraf that the impression I had was one of protection and revelation. The women were clearly survivors of violence and in need of protection and

130

support, but what they revealed through their sharing was their tremendous courage. One young woman there had described how her father had fallen into great debt and sold her to an old man when she was only fourteen years old. Horrified and frightened, she decided to run away. Another woman from an educated, middle-class background told us how her family had condemned her when she fell in love with a man of her choice, accusing her of threatening the family honour. She realized that, even with an education, her family did not respect her right to make decisions about the way she wanted to live her life. She overheard discussions of threats to her life and, afraid to end up dead at the hands of her family as had been the fate of so many women, she escaped to save her life.

Mrs Musharraf listened with compassion and responded, 'It is precisely for women like these that we established the shelter. They deserve protection and an opportunity to live free from fear.' I knew Pakistan was committed to this issue through the work that UNIFEM had been doing to support the Ministry of Women's Affairs. But after seeing so many cases, I also knew that the problem of violence had to be addressed at a deeper level. I replied, 'It is indeed highly commendable that Pakistan has created these shelters. But shelters alone are not a solution. We need to not only give the girls a place to run to, but to address the reasons why they were forced to run away in the first place.' The problem, indeed, was not just in Pakistan; throughout the world, one of the biggest challenges to ending VAW was the normalization of violence and how it was allowed to be justified by the claims of 'cultural values' and 'traditions'. Ending violence was not just about providing safety for women. It was about changing laws, reforming justice systems so that perpetrators could be properly prosecuted, and, most importantly, changing the way women were valued and treated throughout societies.

Through my work in so many countries, I came to realize that violence against women and girls was a global problem, one that many communities accepted or, at least, tolerated, and one that was addressed primarily as a private matter. Out of fear, shame and self-blame, deep silences marked the lives of too many women and girls who lived through violence. They kept their silence because VAW was often an unpunished crime. Violence in families, workplaces, and institutions was carefully hidden, covered by lies and by powers that guarded their dark secrets. Throughout the world, unspeakable violence stigmatized women and girls, robbed them of their agency and dignity, and pushed them to the fringes to deal with their inner trauma alone. Women activists had been marching to put this issue on the public policy agenda since the 1970s. But the international community was resistant and regarded VAW largely as a private matter that did not merit the attention of governments or the UN system. At the beginning of the UN World Decade for Women (1976–85) the issue of VAW was not even on the agenda of the decade that called for equality, development, and peace. It was not even included in the 1979 CEDAW. It was time to break the silence that kept the dirty secret of VAW hidden from the international attention it deserved.

Out of the Shadows

Violence against women was pulled out of the dark shadows of the private realm into the public light by the global women's movement. The opportunity came during the UN World Conference on Human Rights (1993), the International Conference on Population and Development (1994), and the FWCW (1995). Women across the globe showed that VAW was not simply random individual acts of misconduct. It was widespread and deeply rooted in unequal power relationships and pervasive discrimination against women. At the 1993 World Conference on Human Rights, the interaction between women's advocacy, political leaders and various UN partners became the driving force in establishing VAW as a human rights issue. This was not an easy task. Even in UNIFEM, there was little interest in the issue throughout the eighties as VAW was not seen as a development concern, until a UNIFEM staff, Roxanna Carrillo, a feminist leader from Peru produced a powerful paper entitled, 'Violence Against Women: An Obstacle to Development' in 1991. To me, this was not surprising, as at the founding of the UN itself there was a separation between the 'public' and the 'private' spheres with national governments, which were coming out of colonialism, demanding sovereignty on matters regarded as 'private' such as family formation, marriage, and cultural practices. The UN was not supposed to be involved in these issues except that women globally were mobilizing, using the UN conferences of the nineties to change practices and behaviours that were jeopardizing their lives. By making the link between VAW and the significant costs to development, allowed UNIFEM as a UN development fund to legitimately take on the issue. Soon after, within the UN, UNIFEM became a major ally of women's organizations, financing and supporting their work of organizing for the World Conference on Human Rights in Vienna. Finally, the 1993 UN Declaration on the Elimination of Violence against Women became the first international human rights instrument to deal specifically with VAW. It affirmed that VAW contravenes human rights, and it made states and the international community accountable to international norms and standards. Other world conferences that followed made the link between eliminating violence and women's progress unquestionably clear.

In the lead-up to the Beijing Conference, as the world prepared for the largest world conference on women ever held, data on the wide-ranging and intersecting forms of violence that women face in every country began to proliferate in ways we had never seen before. Women and girls had long been subjected to violence in a wide range of settings, including within the family, community, workplace, sports, religious institutions, state custody, and armed conflicts. The multiple forms of violence, including intimate partner violence, incest, female genital mutilation, so-called honour killings, acid attacks, child marriage, and sex trafficking were shocking, as were their numbers. According to Nobel Laureate and economist Amartya Sen, roughly eighty million women who should be living today in China and India are 'missing' because of female infanticide. Women in both the Global North and South live at risk of physical harm in ways and on a scale that have no direct parallel for men. Research indicated that in the United States, a woman is physically abused by her intimate partner every 9 seconds. Female genital mutilation affects an estimated 100 million women worldwide, and every day, 6,000 girls are genitally mutilated to control their sexuality. Each year, two million girls between ages five and fifteen are forced into the commercial sex market. In India, more than 5,000 women are killed each year in notorious 'dowry deaths'. In Pakistan, according to the Human Rights Commission of Pakistan (HRCP), there were about 1,100 honour killings of women by family members in 2015 alone while many more cases went unreported. And an estimated 50,000 women and girls were raped in Bosnia-Herzegovina during the war in the Balkans.[17]

Behind every number, there was a painful story of the impact of violence on the real lives of women and girls. I became a witness

---

[17]   Statistics quoted are from the UN Human Development Report, UNDP, 1995, prepared for the FWCW; 'The Intolerable Status Quo: Violence against Women and Girls' in Progress of Nations, UNICEF 1997; 'Women in Transition', UNICEF, 1999; and 'The State of the World's Population', UNFPA, 2000.

to many women who told their stories at the tribunals that were organized, and in the many countries I visited before and after the Beijing conference as the Executive Director of UNIFEM. The unveiling of secrets was as painful and shocking as it was courageous. Legal systems that covered up for abusers and pardoned rapists if they were willing to marry their victims; fathers who committed incest and then lie to discredit daughters bleeding in pain, but too young to understand what was happening to them; mothers who were willing to sell their daughters to rich, older men to survive or repay a debt; the Catholic Church's long-running saga of priests who sexually abused young boys and girls, and the church hierarchy that protected them; and family members murdering daughters in the name of family honour and then being legally pardoned if forgiven by a relative. Women felt attacked from within their own family, their society, and the patriarchal powers that kept the conspiracy of silence.

The FWCW encouraged many women from all over the world to break their silence, raising issues that others overlooked and seeking to end abuses that others accepted. I was at the parallel NGO forum on Women held in Huairou, 35 miles north of Beijing and an hour away from the official site where the governments were meeting. Despite the heavy rain and the muddy fields, it was the largest gathering of women sponsored by the UN. Huge cheers by women from civil society greeted then First Lady of the United States Hillary Clinton when she came to amplify the slogan 'women's rights are human rights' that the women's movements had been advancing.

Responding to the Pandemic

Building on the momentum of the UN world conferences, UNIFEM's directors in Latin America and the Caribbean were quick to respond to the call of diverse women's movements at the front lines. In 1997, they initiated a series of UN system-wide regional campaigns—'Lives Free of Violence: It's Our Right'. These campaigns advocated for better support to survivors and placed their needs and perspectives at the heart of our action. To prevent future violence, they supported member states to revise discriminatory laws, introduce new legislation, strengthen enforcement, educate and change mindsets, and mobilize more sectors of the population around this issue globally. At its launch, a journalist asked me: 'Do you really believe that a problem as common and as widespread as violence against women can be brought to an end?' My response was a definite 'yes'. Yes, because I believed the pandemic of violence could be stopped. Yes, because I believed that there were women and men around the world who dared to imagine a world free of VAW and embark on creating it.

UNIFEM's work in convening the campaigns immediately brought together ten UN funds, programmes and agencies, and secured endorsement of nineteen governments to revise the national legislation to end VAW. It was a constructive collaboration with member states and a unified alliance that unleashed the full potential of the UN system on this critical issue. It demonstrated how multilateral commitments were converted into action to deliver hope and new possibilities in an area that was previously considered taboo. Within four months, it generated so much interest and action that UNIFEM's programme directors in Africa, Asia-Pacific, Central and Eastern Europe, and the Commonwealth of Independent States replicated the effort with campaigns that reflected regional realities. Together, the campaigns placed the issue of VAW on the agendas of governments worldwide, forging new partnerships and raising awareness in the media, educational institutions, and the public and private sectors. Each regional campaign highlighted regional-specific manifestations of VAW and informed the public at large about the harmful ramifications to not just women but also to the society as a whole.

In almost every region of the world, we mobilized some of the best advertising agencies working with women survivors and women's civil society to design public media campaigns to reach the hearts and minds of the public. Powerful messages on ending VAW were highly visible in public spaces through posters, recognizable slogans, and public service announcements in local languages on hundreds of radio stations and television channels. Campaigns were endorsed by prominent personalities—both men and women—information flyers distributed in popular magazines, and a diverse range of public events, including press conferences, public dialogues, debates, and photography contests, were held. Actors Glenn Close, Dana Reeve, and Julie Andrews graced several key events to lend their support, and Nicole Kidman became our Goodwill Ambassador, travelling with me to Kosovo and highlighting the work of our Trust Fund to End Violence against Women. South African President Nelson Mandela became our strongest advocate, and several influential male leaders championed the issues in the work of their institutions. The Executive Director of UNAIDS, Dr Peter Piot, incorporated the urgent need to address gender-based violence to stem the spread of HIV/AIDs. James Wolfensohn, president of the World Bank, committed the World Bank to addressing VAW as a priority in its investment of specific projects as well as a component in sectors such as transport, education, and social protection, often partnering with UNIFEM on how to do so effectively. All these efforts helped to establish an environment that was conducive for preventing, raising awareness, and ending VAW. They awakened the consciousness of millions throughout the world to gender-based violence, mobilizing new constituencies and generating strengthened political will, with women in politics working across party lines to prioritize this issue.

The campaigns also served to underline the concrete actions that had to be taken at regional, national, and community levels to address the problem. In the immediate term, the priority was to ensure that prevention and protection mechanisms were in place to ensure the safety of women and girls, strengthen the legal system to bring perpetrators to justice, and offer medical and legal remedies to survivors. In the longer term, the challenge was to change entrenched attitudes, gender stereotypes, and power structures that were at the root of the pandemic. By involving UN country teams, governments, and civil society, we increased the chance that VAW was included in the country assistance agreement with the UN and, eventually, with the World Bank and Regional Development Banks. A particularly vital initiative of the campaign was the involvement of local governments and communities and establishing exchange and cooperation programmes among Latin American municipalities on redesigning public spaces and local transport systems.

Through UNIFEM's efforts and my visits to various countries, it was clear that more support and resources needed to be in the hands of women organizing to end VAW. To further support the mobilization, global activism, and campaigns, I took charge and worked with the United Nations General Assembly to establish a United Nations Trust Fund in Support of Actions to Eliminate Violence against Women in 1996. The creation of the trust fund was possible because of the generous support of several governments, including Japan and the United States, and private foundations. It became the first global mechanism devoted exclusively to provide new financial resources, catalysing and supporting concrete programmes on the ground. The aim was to fund innovative and catalytic projects that were strategically placed to have impact and contribute to learning about the most effective strategies for eliminating VAW. The projects the trust fund focused on included a wide range of innovative initiatives in the area of education, capacity-building, violence prevention and deterrence, awareness in raising and the reversal of ingrained attitudes, and action-oriented research. With this, we were able to further bolster the momentum and advocacy efforts undertaken through the campaigns.

The trust fund helped to forge partnerships with new constituencies, including youth and men's groups united to find solutions to specific problems. We were able to finance and link many local initiatives to national efforts and the global movement against violence. We could show the results of this effort, community by community, region by region. For example, in the Caribbean, women's crisis centres began to work with police departments to improve their response to cases of VAW. In Colombia, health professionals were being taught to identify cases of violent abuse as well as reporting and counselling skills. In Jordan, the media broke the traditional silence on the crime of 'honour killings' of women suspected of adultery. The issue was subsequently championed by our Goodwill Ambassador, Princess Basma, and discussed in parliament. In Ethiopia, women community leaders were trained as paralegals to provide legal counselling to women. In Senegal, a groundbreaking law banning female genital mutilation was implemented and, together with the help of religious leaders, a campaign to educate the public on the harmful consequences of the practice was launched. In Latin America, UNIFEM offices came together to initiate safe cities in seven countries, working with municipalities and urban planners to identify unsafe neighbourhoods and public areas, design new safety plans, and improve street lighting and public transport to improve safety for women and girls and the quality of life for all in the communities.

The 1993 World Conference on Human Rights in Vienna and the 1995 FWCW in Beijing made a big difference in the way VAW was dealt with at the global level. For the first time, VAW was seen in the context of women's human rights, not simply as a private matter. Before the Beijing conference, the issue was so marginalized that even CEDAW did not include VAW as a discrimination to be eliminated. And, it was because women around the world, through their institutions and movements, were able to work on powerful and effective campaigns to change people's mindsets and create a deep understanding of the issues, that eventually VAW was included in the CEDAW protocol. Equally important was the legitimacy given to women's groups around the world as leaders of the global movement, together with some mainstream political leaders forming part of this specific coalition. The women's movement and UNIFEM now wanted to seriously discuss the issue of state accountability for ending VAW—one of the big achievements at the Vienna Human Rights Conference and the FWCW. Violence was not just something to be dealt with by women for women; it was something that the states had to seriously take accountability for and it was essential that they took on the primary responsibility to end impunity. To implement this commitment, we needed to address this not state-by-state, but as a global multilateral network of powerful member states, male and female leaders, civil society, and the UN system interacting to formulate meaningful ideas for decision-making. Hence, we needed the strongest support and collective power of the UN General Assembly.

Women's Voices in the UN General Assembly

For me, ending violence in women's lives was one of the most transformational agendas for the twenty-first century, requiring political courage and decisive action from all our leaders to move from commitment to implementation. With successes on the ground, it was time to bring the voices of women survivors to the global stage, to share the outcomes of the UN campaigns and showcase some of the successful strategies the trust fund was supporting. My team and I decided to organize a major UN multimedia conference in the UN General Assembly (UNGA) on the last International Women's Day of the twentieth century. There was resistance from DAW as the theme for the Commission on the Status of Women for that year was 'women's health'. Their leadership felt that focusing on VAW would embarrass member states and distract from the agenda of the commission. Their senior human rights adviser who participated in our interagency organizing group said to me, 'What has violence against women got to do with women's health?' It was unsettling to realize how fragmented we were in our understanding and the approaches used by the Secretariat and the operational agencies. Finally, we could only proceed because of strong support from Dr Nafis Sadik, executive director of the United Nations Fund for Population Affairs (UNFPA); Ambassador Stephen Lewis, deputy executive director of UNICEF; and Elisabeth Lindenmayer from the Executive Office of the UN secretary general, and the tenacity and creativity of my team led by Joanne Sandler.

The thought of mobilizing the General Assembly as a whole grew from my discussions with Bella Abzug, the iconic former congresswoman and women's human rights leader who had become one of our strongest supporters. She suggested the idea to capture the space of the General Assembly as a symbolic act of power and use it as a platform of global authority from which to mobilize the member states. The idea was not to single out member states, but rather create a global tide of change, with the global women's movement as its driving force, galvanizing action from member states to implement their commitments on the issue. Thus, the vision of UNIFEM's global videoconference, 'A World Free of Violence against Women', came into being.

For the first time in the history of the UN, thousands of women and men, young and old, gathered in the UNGA on International Women's Day—8 March 1999—for the global videoconference. The event celebrated some of the most inspiring stories about the fight against violence by extraordinary women around the world. Spearheaded by UNIFEM in coordination with many other UN organizations, the event linked government leaders, top UN decision-makers, and advocates in the General Assembly by satellite to tens of thousands of people located in five sites in Africa, Asia, Latin America, and Europe. Women shared their experience from the trust fund and the many successful community-, national- and global-level initiatives that were achieving the goal of eliminating all forms of VAW, and leaders learned of successful examples that could be replicated and upscaled across the regions. Several women ambassadors were so inspired that they immediately took leadership in the 1999 UNGA to establish the International Day for the Elimination of Violence against Women. On 17 December 1999, the General Assembly unanimously agreed and designated 25 November as the International Day for the Elimination of Violence against Women through GA Resolution 54/134. This date marks the assassination of the Mirabel sisters in the Dominican Republic and now, every year, it starts the global '16 Days of Activism' that precedes Human Rights Day on 10 December. At about the same time, the CEDAW Optional Protocol that allowed individual women to bring complaints of 'grave and systematic violations' and hold states accountable was unanimously adopted by the General Assembly on 6 October 1999.

With the support of the UN Secretary General Kofi Annan, the president of the World Bank, James Wolfensohn, and iconic leaders such as President Nelson Mandela at the videoconference, we were able to harness the highest political will to generate historic commitments. They focused on key areas from the trust fund and the campaigns that could together accelerate change, but required greater attention and investment. These were: the need to support research and documentation, strengthen our evidence base, and understanding; the need to review legislation and adopt UN frameworks to criminalize gender-based violence and end impunity; the need to scale up the provision of appropriate and affordable support services to support survivors; the need to create community responsibility for and education of the importance of ending VAW in all societies; the need to change institutional attitudes, including training law-enforcement agencies, the judiciary, healthcare providers, educators, religious leaders, and the media; and changing male behaviour and emergence of male champions working alongside women to end violence.

That same year, in late 1999, I was invited to give the keynote address at the Toronto White Ribbon Campaign, commemorating the first International Day to End Violence against Women. It would have been unimaginable just a few years ago to have men striving to end VAW. But that day, the Royal York's Canadian Ballroom was packed with over 1,100 people. The occasion was upbeat with the mayor proclaiming November 25 to December 10 as official White Ribbon days, and Jack Layton, co-chair of the White Ribbon campaign, reminding us that every man who pins on a white ribbon is pledging 'never to commit, condone, or remain silent about violence against women'. It was time that men acknowledged and addressed the pandemic that has destroyed the lives of so many women and girls. The White Ribbon campaign is one of the inspiring initiatives that upheld the principle that VAW was not a 'women's issue', but a human rights issue, and that stopping it required shared responsibility and joint commitment by everyone in society.

Secretary General Kofi Annan as a Champion

Years prior to our global videoconference, I had the privilege of meeting Kofi Annan in 1994 when he was the UN Under-Secretary-General for peace operations. On most mornings, we would take the cable car across the East River from our homes on Roosevelt Island and walk from East 60th Street to the United Nations building. He was a good listener, always wanting to learn about the work we were doing with women in conflict-affected countries, from Liberia and Kosovo to East Timor.

When Kofi Annan became the secretary general of the UN, my first encounter with him as the executive director of the UN Women's Development Fund (UNIFEM) involved addressing VAW. In 1997, when he was elected, this was not an issue that the UN was comfortable addressing with great visibility in New York. The discomfort first became clear when I organized a black-and-white photo exhibit in the General Assembly lobby, called 'Wall of Shame, Wall of Hope', which included graphic images of women from different cultures being subjected to abuse. I had invited Nane Annan to open the exhibit, and some people around the secretary general raised an alarm arguing that his wife, Nane, should not go because the photos were controversial and would embarrass member states. On the day of the opening, Kofi went down to look at the photos himself, concluding that our governments needed to assume greater responsibility to end the shameful violation of women. The Wall of Hope showed what governments could do, and what some governments were already doing. Nane opened the exhibition, which was a big success as part of the campaign to end VAW. I was made aware of this incident at the opening itself and was touched that the UN secretary general took the time to investigate the matter for himself. He later wrote me two letters to express his 'delight' to learn about the UN-wide interagency campaign and express his 'full support' for the global videoconference that UNIFEM was planning. He continued to say, 'I am particularly pleased that you have chosen to take advantage of the new communication technologies that are shaping our world and making possible a kind of diplomacy, solidarity and coordinated action unthinkable just a few years ago.'

The 1999 multimedia videoconference used the latest satellite technology for the first time to link five sites around the world to the UNGA. In preparation for it, UNIFEM had also explored the use of new information and communication technologies (ICTs) for their potential in reducing VAW. We started an electronic conversation on the Internet, with the support of the World Bank and Global Knowledge Partnership, and facilitated by the Educational Development Centre (a project of Harvard and Massachusetts Institute of Technology). This brought together groups from around the globe to exchange strategies against violence that worked. Thousands of women and men shared their experiences on a daily listserv, as well as their determination, courage, and energy. We believed that as ICTs would become more available, they could be used to obtain information on model legislation, training modules and exchange of experiences, data, and resources. An interactive site with information resources and where strategies to address VAW were shared could further advance these issues in the national and international arena.

I wanted the UN secretary general to be our guest of honour at the videoconference. Again, some of his bureaucratic advisers told him to stay away, as the topic was too controversial for many governments. Eventually, I was informed that if the secretary general came, it would only be for three minutes. Kofi listened to his advisers, but he made up his own mind. Not only did he attend, he was also so taken by the whole event that he stayed for over an hour listening intensely and was deeply moved. In 2001, when he was awarded the Conrad Hilton Humanitarian Prize of $100,000, he donated the full amount to the UN Trust Fund to End Violence against Women. I knew that Secretary General Kofi Annan wanted to do so much more for women, especially those affected by the greatest crisis of the time, HIV/AIDs—a major priority on his agenda. However, there were far too many serious pressures that deeply troubled him—from Washington's failure to abide by international law resulting in the war in Iraq that he classified as 'illegal', to accusations of corruption in the Oil-for-Food programme established by the UN that allowed Iraq to sell oil in exchange for food and other humanitarian needs for ordinary citizens. He was most affected emotionally by the 2003 bombing of the UN office in Baghdad, Iraq, that wounded over 100 and killed twenty-two UN staff members, including his Special Representative and close friend, Sergio de Mello. It was with great sadness that I watched him caught in the political crosshairs between superpowers forcing him to be more disengaged from the affairs of the UN he loved. He will always remain our champion.

Navigating the Danger Zones

After our successful multimedia videoconference, UNIFEM's work on violence continued to gather strength and credibility, and more governments turned to us for help in combatting VAW as a public issue. In December 2002, I was invited by the First Lady of Mexico, Marta Fox, to visit Ciudad Juárez and recommend possible action to deal with the issue of femicide in one of the most dangerous cities for women in the world. At the time I visited, about 400 women were reported murdered and an estimated 3,000 had been missing since the mid-1990s. Most of these women were young factory workers in the maquiladoras, or manufacturing plants, where free-trade zones provided most of the jobs for the Ciudad Juárez–El Paso border area. The young women were kidnapped, tortured, sexually abused, mutilated, and dumped in the desert or garbage heaps. For years the murders, many speculated as linked to drug cartels and criminal networks, were repeatedly ignored and left unresolved.

I listened to the heart-wrenching testimonies from the mothers of murdered daughters, the relatives of the victims, and female activists working with the families. They complained that despite massive demonstrations and candlelight vigils, there was a lack of proper process of investigation and accountability. According to them, reports had been lost or misplaced and law enforcement and judicial systems were ineffective. They now wanted the government to take full responsibility, address institutional corruption, and end femicide. They demanded better oversight of public institutions, the end of impunity, and justice for the crimes committed. Protected by presidential bodyguards, I visited the impoverished neighbourhoods of the victims and the factories where they worked. The factories, both foreign and locally owned, attracted young migrant workers from different parts of Mexico into their assembly line production as part of the Border Industrialization Program, exporting the majority of the manufactured items to the United States. With bottom-line profit considerations, I discovered that young women workers, including those on night shifts, were locked out of the factories whenever they were late reporting for their shift. They were forced to return home alone in the dark. At the same time, those completing their shifts walked long distances to their homes because the factory buses refused to enter the impoverished areas due to the poor infrastructure of unpaved, unlit streets. I was also informed that factories tended to subcontract bus companies and drivers without proper background checks. All these had endangered the safety of the young women.

I shared my observation with the government at the end of my week-long visit. At the press conference, I stressed that certain actions must be implemented immediately to improve the security and safety of women. Employers must be more accountable for the security of their workers, change their dangerous practices of turning workers away, and ensure better screening of their bus drivers. I called on the federal government to take a greater role in the investigations and the functioning of the law-enforcement and criminal justice systems, which were being handled largely by the northern state of Chihuahua. I expressed my deepest admiration for the work of local women groups and mothers of murdered daughters to highlight the issues and demand accountability, sometimes at the risk of their own safety. The forces that create environments where VAW thrives, such as in Ciudad Juárez, often seem insurmountable. But, because of the global movement to make VAW unacceptable, we have seen the emergence of new political will in so many parts of the globe to condemn and address such violence as a serious human rights violation that had to end and mobilize state institutions towards that common purpose.

Women Changing Power

When we started our work and had a dedicated UN Trust Fund to End Violence Against Women, I could never have imagined that today, VAW would be accepted as universally devastating, the most serious violation of women's human rights that transcends all boundaries. It is on the world's political agenda and is being addressed at national, regional, and international levels. Its exorbitant human and economic costs are being calculated. The World Bank estimates that VAW is as serious a cause of death and incapacity among women as cancer, and a greater cause of ill health than traffic accidents and malaria combined. It has now committed to addressing gender-based violence through investment and collaboration with women around the world. The World Health Organization (WHO) indicates that one in every three women worldwide has experienced violence in her lifetime, most often by someone she knows.[18] It has started a curriculum for training healthcare professionals to provide care for women subjected to violence.

I could have never imagined that through our work with governments, today there is a better understanding that VAW is a critical concern for development, our societies, and our own humanity. There is greater commitment that attitudes and behaviors, laws and policies need to change and high-quality services for survivors provided to address the pandemic of violence that affects every nation, class, race, and religion. These changes happened because we invested in empowering women and knew how to use the UNGA as a space to gain rights and protection for women. We dared to demand accountability and assembled our governments at the global videoconference to hear empowered women's voices narrating how 'the personal is political' and 'it is not cultural, it is criminal'. Women shared their stories of how the impact of violence, especially at home, directly destroyed their security, health, and mental and emotional well-being. Their physical and less-visible psychological injuries, and their shame

---

[18] World Health Organization, 'Global and Regional Estimates of Violence against Women: Prevalence and Health Effects of Intimate Partner Violence and Non-Partner Sexual Violence' (Geneva, 2013).

shrunk the range of choices open to women and girls, narrowing their options in almost every sphere of life, public and private—at home, in school, in the workplace, and in their community. It eroded their self-confidence and filled them with despair. In short, violence has left far too many women and girls disempowered, with disrupted lives and destroyed talents, damaging their future possibilities. It is criminal and a mark of shame on all our societies.

In advancing our work to address VAW, we must always keep our eyes on emerging trends that intensify or create new forms of violence and their impact on women. While many women have now fought back against those who use physical, emotional, and professional power to abuse them, we are, unfortunately, also witnessing new threats to human and global security. The growing influence of extremist national and transnational forces are working to close down democratic spaces and mobilize against the ethos of our society, against human rights, especially women's human rights. In many parts of the world, the gains made to improve women's lives are now under attack or have been lost because of growing intolerance, violent extremism, protracted conflicts, humanitarian crises, and the impact of the global health pandemic. Today, we are challenged by the rise of ethnonationalism, the spread of hate speech in cyberspace helping to fuel xenophobia, divisive politics, racism, and narrow self-interest that have deepened social fractures and threaten to weaken the multilateral norms and institutions that promote tolerance, justice, and collective global interest.

At this fragile moment of shifting global political rivalry combined with the grievances and anger of people affected by multiple health, socio-economic and political crises and the misuse of new technologies, we need to be persistent in seeking and forging collaborative relationships to shape a wider framework of global stability and human security. Our world needs nothing less than a new global social contract with a protection floor of fundamental rights, especially for people struggling against persecution and the violation of human dignity. Women must be at the centre of this social contract, raising their voices, demanding accountability, leading change, building effective coalitions, pressuring institutions, and creating a vision of a world free from violence and fear for everyone. For in the words of Bela Abzug, 'Women will change the nature of power, rather than the nature of power changing women.'

7

Women, Peace, and Security

'True peace is not merely the absence of war, it is the presence of justice.'

—Jane Addams

In 1996, a few years before our UNIFEM videoconference, I visited the town of Arusha in northern Tanzania as part of an official visit to East Africa, accompanied by my twin daughters. Long serving as the gateway to Mount Kilimanjaro and the Serengeti, since November 1994, Arusha became home to an institution that embodied one of the darkest chapters of history—the International Criminal Tribunal for Rwanda (ICTR).

UNIFEM had started working in Rwanda soon after the genocide through its regional programme on African Women in Crisis. The genocide in Rwanda took place in the context of the Rwandan Civil War and a long colonial history of 'divide and rule' that had entrenched racialized identities of Hutu as 'indigenous' and Tutsi as 'foreigner'. In April 1994, a plane carrying the then presidents of Rwanda and Burundi was shot down over Kigali. The incident killed both leaders and shattered the Arusha Accords that had been signed in 1993, and was followed by a wave of genocidal mass killings targeting the Tutsi minority that left an estimated 800,000 people dead and millions displaced within 100 days.

After arriving in Arusha, I was taken to see the court chambers, where testimonies of genocide survivors and witnesses were given. As I entered the building, a chill ran through me, and I asked myself, 'How would this humble institution be able to bring justice to those who survived the worst genocides of modern times?' Inside the court building, I met with several female survivors and witnesses so that I could hear from them directly about their experiences as well as the support they needed from us. One woman told me how she and hundreds of others had sought safety and hid in a church. It was soon broken into and she was caught and beaten, and then brutally gang-raped by a group of men. While many people were killed before her eyes, for some reason that she could not comprehend, her life was spared. Being one of the few to survive and bearing the shame of rape, she told me that she wished that she had died that day. What was most painful for her was that many of the killers and rapists were people she knew, including neighbours with whom she had shared meals and friendships. Indeed, it was the familiarity between victims and killers that made the nature of violence in the Rwandan genocide so difficult to accept. People were killed in their neighbourhood streets, churches, and schools, and even in their own homes. No place was safe, there was nowhere to run to, and everyone was an enemy. The killers were not cold-blooded militia, but teachers, doctors, and priests from the same communities as their victims.

The genocide affected women and men in different ways. While men made up the majority of the victims of the killings, women suffered from the use of rape as a weapon of genocide and mass violence. According to the then UN Special Rapporteur on Rwanda, Rene Degni-Segui, between 250,000 and 500,000 women and girls were estimated to have been raped between April and July 1994. Rape was the rule, and its absence the exception, he wrote in his 1996 report. Rape was used to dehumanize and destroy the Tutsi people, stripping them not only of their dignity, but also of their identity. The methods of genocidal rape took many brutal forms. Women were raped in public, often outside their homes, in front of their family members and communities. Women who were not killed after being raped were often tortured with mutilation of genitalia, reproductive organs and features that were perceived to be defining of their ethnicity. Rape was also conducted with the intention of forced impregnation as well as infection of HIV. Women who were not killed were forced into marriage and sexual slavery with the genocidaires.

The agony of the horrific stories that the women told me was only deepened by the deficiencies and inequalities that I saw within the court itself. I was shocked to learn that most of the judges at the criminal court were male and that these judges were provided with tight security, while the women who came forward to testify had none. It seemed that even the accused had better living facilities than the women witnesses. The women, on the other hand, who had come forward with extraordinary courage to confront their abusers despite their shame, were given next to no protection or trauma support. They sacrificed their time with their children and their means of livelihood to come all the way to Arusha to testify, risking their safety and reliving their ordeals in the hope that some justice would be served. And to make matters worse, even though voices of witnesses were distorted, some of them were still identified and targeted upon return to Rwanda.

The next morning, I experienced something that I never had before. I felt an extreme pain in my legs and had great difficulty standing up and walking. My daughters, Lilianne and Pauline, stayed by my side, and kept asking me, 'What happened, Mum?' To which I could only answer, 'I am in pain, I can't walk . . .' Far from being caused by any physical condition, I soon realized that this pain was a psychosomatic reaction to what I had heard and

seen the day before. Since the previous night, I had felt myself
bleeding for the Rwandan women I had met, and the millions
whom I had not met. And now it was an acute sense of disbelief,
anger, and helplessness that paralysed me, mirroring the paralysis
that I felt the international community, UN, and its Security
Council displayed in the face of mass inhumanity on such an
immense scale. How was this possible, I asked myself? Wasn't this
kind of violence exactly what the UN was created to prevent? I felt
that morning that what I was bearing witness to was not merely a
weak criminal court with inadequate protection for women, but a
systemic failure of the international community and the UN itself
to protect women from the worst forms of violence. That morning,
I decided that I had to do something. I could not let the UN fail
these women nor the communities they were holding together.

With my UNIFEM team, we designed a programme that
provided women with witness protection and trauma counselling.
We also saw that it was the women who were weaving back
together the fabric of their tattered societies, sowing the seeds
of forgiveness within communities divided by hatred, blame,
and unspeakable acts of violence, where the soil was still heavy
with the spilt blood of parents, children, and neighbours of all
sides. These were the bonds that had to be invested in, for they
offered the possibility of restoring humanity where it had been
forgotten. Through UNIFEM, we supported a wide range of
transformative programmes, from a successful livelihoods project
with HIV-infected women weaving their peace baskets which we
introduced to the US market, to the training of women leaders
for parliament.

On the same trip, I also met a close colleague, Navi Pillay,
now newly appointed as judge and president at the ICTR.
Navi was a formidable and courageous jurist who had defended
anti-apartheid activists and was appointed by President Nelson

Mandela as the first non-white woman to serve on the High Court of South Africa. She understood the criminal and politicized nature of rape in the Rwandan genocide and upheld the need for accountability. We discussed the challenges of dealing with sexual violence against women as crime that was used systematically as a weapon of genocide. I came to realize that the problem was not only the inadequate number of female judges and weak witness protection at the ICTR itself, but also the lack of an international legal framework to deal with rape as a war crime and a set of legally binding norms and standards specifically on women and armed conflict.

And so, in the aftermath of the genocide and in pursuit of justice for the women whose lives had been torn apart by it, we decided that we needed to build a global movement to legally recognize rape and sexual violence as a weapon of war. UNIFEM joined forces with many women's organizations, in Africa and beyond, to mobilize at national, regional, and global levels, and Rwanda remained at the forefront as the case upon which a precedent could be established. In 1998, we had a major success. Jean Paul Akayesu, the mayor of Taba commune, had been indicted for fifteen counts of genocide and crimes against humanity. Initially, rape was not included in the charges, but was later added to the charges, thanks to persistent advocacy and mobilization from women's groups across Africa and internationally. On 2 September 1998, Akayesu became the first person to be ever convicted for the use of rape as a form of genocide, making the ICTR the first international tribunal to define rape in international criminal law and recognize it as a means of perpetrating genocide. The Akayesu judgement was historic and it set judicial precedent not only for the Rwanda tribunal but also for rape and sexual violence to be prosecuted under international law as an act of genocide and crime against humanity.

As I visited more war-torn countries, it became clearer to me that the horrifying VAW in Rwanda was not an isolated case. Neither was this a problem that was contained to any one continent. A year after my visit to Arusha, I visited Srebrenica in Bosnia and spoke to women who were survivors of ethnic cleansing. Again, I heard terrifying stories from women of mass rape and humiliation, of women who were forcibly impregnated as a tactic of war. I met women and girls who had been detained in what they referred to as 'rape camps', repeatedly raped while in detention, often gang-raped by large groups and often in public. Those who became pregnant were kept in detention until the time of delivery. There were also those who were forced into sexual slavery and made to provide services to soldiers at the army camps or face death. And this brutality had taken place in the heart of Europe, the very continent whose devastation in the two world wars spurred the creation of the UN itself. I began to realize that what was needed was an enforceable legal framework at the global peace and security level. The only level that could achieve this was the United Nations Security Council. In discussions with local women and civil society organizations, women affected by war told me that they felt that the Security Council was not doing enough, that it talked about peace and security but was not thinking about women as part of that agenda. The UN was used to engaging governments, but did not always recognize community leadership. Many women were trying to hold their communities together, but their leadership was not recognized or supported.

Since my appointment, UNIFEM had provided assistance to women in conflict-affected countries and supported their participation in local peace processes. But, our efforts were marginalized and local women's groups organizing in conflict-affected countries were not taken seriously at all by the major UN entities involved with peace and security. In fact, our complaints of sexual violence by peacekeepers at that time were regarded with suspicion and I was even told by an Under-Secretary-General that we were undermining the UN by bringing it up. When I complained about witnessing some peacekeepers soliciting scantily-clad young women lining the road when I arrived early one morning in Liberia during curfew hours, the response from the Special Representative of the Secretary General (SRSG) was how else would one expect the young women to earn a livelihood. It shocked me that sexual servicing was regarded as normal, and that some senior officials did not understand the principles, norms, and standards of the UN. And it angered me that some UN peacekeepers were exploiting their power over the vulnerability of these girls, without any sense that their behaviour was exploitative, much less any sense of accountability, nor of the damage they were doing to all serving under the UN flag.

In 2000, several women leaders and civil society activists whom we supported in conflict-affected countries, together with International Alert, approached me to ask if I could take leadership from the UN side and help prepare the ground for the first Security Council Resolution addressing women, peace, and security. A tremendous opportunity had opened up to move the agenda, as Namibia had expressed interest to address the issue of women in conflict-affected countries during its presidency of the Security Council in October 2000. After the gender and peacekeeping seminar organized in Windhoek, Namibia, in May 2000, the country wanted to sponsor a resolution that was impactful for women on the ground, given its own history of struggle. However, there was much work to be done, politically and substantively, to build understanding and consensus to move towards a new paradigm of peace and security. They stressed that UNIFEM had the trust of both member states and civil society as well as knowledge of the realities of women in conflict zones.

I knew the urgency of this and decided that UNIFEM should play a leading role, sharing our experience and in bringing women affected by war directly to the UN Security Council to demand better international protection and accountability from the multilateral system. I decided to take up the challenge despite resistance and interagency rivalry from the UN's fragmented gender entities. I was told that UNIFEM belonged to the development arm of the UN and had no business dealing with the peace and security pillar. Yet, as a person who had devoted much of my professional life to economic security and rights, I knew that in so many countries development gains could be quickly lost if we did not find ways of linking peace and security to development agendas. Furthermore, instead of ideological Cold War divides, ethnic identity and the local distribution of power and resources were now fuelling the conflicts with disastrous consequences at community level, especially for women, who were violently attacked sexually for being reproducers of ethnic identity. Thus, I ignored my detractors and decided to take the opportunity of the UN's agenda for the new millennium with its renewed sense of mission to develop the new Security Council resolution.

A Global Framework for Women, Peace, and Security (SCR1325)

My team and I, working closely with our partners, spent the year preparing the ground through intense consultation and dialogue with key members of the Security Council and with their ministers in their capitals. It was widely felt at the time that there was an insufficient understanding of the realities of women's daily lives in conflict zones and the nature of ethnic conflicts with its politics of ethno-religious identities targeting women's sexuality and reproductive capability. There was, hence, a lack of urgency of what needed to change. In my engagement with the Security Council members during those months, I made it a point to bring women's realities and urgent requests to the highest level of decision-making in the UN. I shared how in every conflict-affected region, I had met women choked with painful experiences and memories of their own humiliation and those of their loved ones—husbands, brothers, daughters, and sons. From the Colombian women in the valley of the widows, to the Bosnian women who were mass raped, to the Tutsi and Hutu women raped and infected with HIV/AIDs in Rwanda and whose tears could not stop when they broke their silence in my arms. Bearing their stories, I emphasized that this dehumanization must stop and that the protection for women and girls in conflict must be addressed at the highest level of the UN—the Security Council. Equally important, based on UNIFEM's experience, my team and I wanted members of the Security Council to realize that women, despite the horrors inflicted on them, were not just victims in times of war. Many were engaged in building peace locally and had important perspectives that could contribute to what a peaceful, secure, and just society should look like. They were, therefore, part of the solution in the transition from violence to peace, but this important role needed the acknowledgement and support of the international multilateral system.

The first leader to recognize this was former President Nelson Mandela when he became the mediator of the Burundi peace process at the end of 1999, following the demise of former President of Tanzania, Julius Nyerere. Thanks to President Mandela, women gained their entry point into the peacemaking process. Burundian women had been working for many years in implementing local peace initiatives, supported by UNIFEM, but had consistently been excluded from the formal peace process at the national level. Recognizing that a more inclusive peace process could increase the chances of lasting peace, President Mandela invited women's groups to input into the design of the Arusha Peace and Reconciliation Agreement. Working with UNIFEM and the Mwalimu Nyerere Foundation, President Mandela supported an All-Party Burundi Women's Peace Conference on 17–20 July 2000 in Arusha, Tanzania. Over fifty Burundian women representatives from the nineteen Burundian political parties involved in the peace negotiations attended and together put forward several gender-specific demands. Among these were the inclusion of a women's charter in the constitution, measures to ensure women's security, women's rights to land, inheritance and education, and an end to impunity for sexual violence and gender-based war crimes. The women's recommendations were presented by President Mandela to the nineteen political parties. Twenty-three of the recommendations, including provisions for education and healthcare and access to justice, employment, and inheritance rights, were included in the final peace accord which was eventually signed on 28 August 2000. They became critical components of the country's reconstruction efforts.

As we worked on conflict after conflict, we found that approximately half of the conflict contexts on the Security Council's agenda covering the Sahel and the Great Lake Regions in Africa, for example, could be considered cases of conflict relapse. We tracked the breakdown of ceasefires and peace agreements, as intergroup dynamics became more hostile due to weak governance and state institutions combined with political and economic exclusion. Using concrete examples of UNIFEM's support for women's peace initiatives, I emphasized to the Security Council members the importance of supporting women's agency and leadership in peacebuilding and recovery, and to strongly link their peacemaking at the community level with high-level mediation processes. When it came to peacemaking and recovery, we had witnessed how the formal peacemaking sector was still dominated by men who understood military security and warring elites. They frequently perceived the peace process as ceasefires and the silencing of guns, often at the expense of long-term peace building. Women were, therefore, excluded from their peace table. Instead, warring parties were invited to the peace talks even when ceasefires and peace agreements were violated. Today, we recognize that peace is more than the absence of violence; it is the presence of justice and peacebuilding from the ground up.

We knew that conflicts occurred because of deeply fractured societies, extreme economic and social inequalities, and entrenched discrimination and political systems that excluded people's voices, fragile governance systems, and rampant corruption. If we wanted sustainable peace, we needed to address the roots of conflict which were multidimensional, involving economic, social, and political forces. Resolving conflicts, peacebuilding and state-building, therefore, had to be addressed within a holistic framework that integrated human security, human development, and human rights to deal with the social fractures that fed conflicts. I stressed that inclusive peace processes were more likely to lead to lasting peace. A more balanced group involved in peacemaking could better address the societal grievances that had escalated into conflict and identify the various demands for political, social, and economic change. Including women of diverse backgrounds in the political decision-making processes that brought a country from war to peace would have allowed different perspectives to be articulated in critical discussions about accountable governance and reconciliation leading to better recovery.

I shared how on the ground, securing strong commitments on women and children in peace agreements and post-conflict reconstruction helped to re-establish lives and weave back the social fabric and social cohesion of the community, preventing the recurrence of conflict. Addressing the underlying inequalities and racism that rendered women and girls vulnerable was crucial for shifting to a future that upheld justice, restored confidence, and transformed institutions to provide greater security and support the rebuilding of communities and lives. With so many men killed, I stressed how when women in parliament established equal rights of inheritance to land in Rwanda, women farmers went back to the farms and rapidly revitalized the agricultural economy and food security for the country. I highlighted how disarmament, demobilization and reintegration (DDR) focused on male combatants, forgetting that there were women and girls in the fighting forces who faced a different set of challenges from their male counterparts. I remember to this day the thirteen-year-old child bride I met in the disarmament, demobilization and reintegration camp in Liberia, holding her baby in one arm and refusing to let me go with the other. Looking hard at me, she said, 'Madam, I know they will forget me; I want to go to school too . . . don't forget me; please help me.'

On the first UN Day of this millennium, 24 October 2000, half a century after the birth of the UN Charter, a major opportunity finally arose for me to officially raise the issues at the heart of accountability for human security, justice, and human rights directly to the UN Security Council. I was invited to address the Security Council on the changing nature of conflict, the use of sexual violence as a weapon of war, problems of exclusion and injustice, and the importance of women's perspectives and participation in decision-making to deal with fragile peace and recovery. Based on the expertise that UNIFEM and our partners had developed working on this agenda for several years across many continents, I presented a compelling case on the urgent need for a new global framework on women, peace, and security, and highlighted the areas for urgent action by the Security Council, the UN, and the member states. We shared documentation of how VAW was being used as a weapon of war and employed with impunity, and how the UN was not equipped to respond adequately to the changing nature of conflicts. I raised the importance of conducting a full-scale assessment on the impact of armed conflict on women and the need to develop a new approach to our response to this issue.

If the goal was to build sustainable peace, I argued, it required more diverse and deeper engagement from the rest of society, and women had a critical role to play in shaping the decisions and institutions needed for the emergence of a fairer and inclusive society for the long-term. I warned that the exclusion of a gender perspective from peacebuilding and recovery processes shut down opportunities for the reforms needed and, therefore, weakened the foundations for sustainable peace and security. It removed hope of a better future for girls. Having no female representation during peace negotiations rendered women's grievances unheard and unaddressed. Even when women were included, they were usually on the sidelines, given observer status as a substitute for real participation. This made it particularly difficult for women to engage meaningfully to bring about agreements that would help reduce the inequalities and lack of accountability that were often at the heart of conflict. Given the importance of women's participation in sustaining peace, their exclusion from the peace table and decision-making, therefore, not just impacted the lives of women and girls, their families, and communities, but also impeded their society's efforts for stability as a whole. Against the advice of some senior UN colleagues, I also highlighted the need to hold the UN accountable, starting with recruiting women as the SRSG to conflict-affected countries. In the year 2000, when I addressed the Security Council, there was not a single female SRSG serving in the UN system.

In addition to engaging the Security Council, UNIFEM was also appointed as the technical adviser supporting the president of Security Council, Namibia, as it negotiated the resolution on women, peace, and security. The role of UNIFEM as technical adviser was critical throughout the drafting of the resolution, supporting the work of the 'pen-holder', Aina Iiyambo, special assistant to the foreign minister of Namibia. As technical advisers, we were able to provide language and be the bridge between the real experiences of women and the high level decision-making process of member states in the Security Council. In addition, my team at UNIFEM proudly prepared and facilitated the women who organized for peace and security on the ground to dialogue for the first time as experts with members of the Security Council, using the Arria Formula. Together with our civil society partners, we brought women from Guatemala, Somalia, and Sierra Leone to share their stories with the Security Council members of how they had the most to gain from new opportunities and also the most to lose if fragile communities broke down. It represented a long overdue recognition of their accomplishments and challenges, and convinced the Security Council of the urgency for a strong resolution instead of a presidential statement.

Finally, the Security Council heeded the voices of the women from conflict-affected countries, of member states, and those of us who addressed the Council. On 31 October 2000, it adopted the historic landmark resolution on Women, Peace and Security (SCR 1325). This marked the beginning of the women, peace, and security agenda in the Security Council. The SCR 1325 consisted of four pillars—prevention, protection, participation, peacebuilding and recovery. It broke the silos between human rights, development, peace, and security; addressed sexual violence as a war crime; and promoted women's rights to inheritance, property and land, healthcare, education and employment, as critical for sustaining peace and in the rebuilding of societies. It supported women's meaningful participation in peace and recovery to overturn underlying inequalities and shift to a future that upheld justice, restored confidence, and transformed institutions for greater peace and security. I will always be grateful for the opportunity to address the Security Council on this issue, and to have UNIFEM serve as the technical adviser to the then president of the Security Council, Namibia. The SCR 1325 became the resolution that inspired substantive and widespread action in the whole UN system, in the security sector of our member states, and among advocates for women's human rights. Till today, it is widely regarded as one of the UN's most transformative and legally binding international frameworks that we have created together with civil society and women living in conflict-affected countries.

Bringing SCR 1325 to Afghanistan and Beyond

After the groundbreaking victory, our next challenge was to take the framework on women, peace, and security forward and make it work on the ground. We tested the first implementation of SCR 1325 in a very difficult political context—Afghanistan after the fall of the Taliban. Images and stories of VAW in Afghanistan dominated our television screens and media soon after the September 11 terrorist attack in New York in 2001. The suffering and exclusion of Afghan women—from public execution to their complete removal from social, economic, and political life— provoked international outrage. For me, the outrage was a sign that the world finally understood that the condition of women in a country is the barometer of peace and security and associated with better governance and functioning states. This was the message of SCR 1325.

I was thrilled when the UN Secretary General Kofi Annan invited me to be part of his delegation to the International Conference on Reconstruction Assistance to Afghanistan in Tokyo in January 2002, hosted by Madam Sadako Ogata, president of the Japan International Cooperation Agency (JICA). The SRSG, Lakhdar Brahimi, had the overall authority for the political, human rights, recovery, and reconstruction activities of the UN in the post-Taliban transition of Afghanistan. He was in the midst of solidifying the 2001 Bonn Agreement that created the Afghan Government. With all the difficulties of bringing stability, self-rule, and security to the country that he had to handle, he strongly advised me to postpone the issue of gender equality and women's empowerment to some future date in the hope that it would be less complicated and easier to handle. He felt that I had not even visited the country and did not fully understand the complexity of the local situation or even what local women really wanted. On my side, with UNIFEM's experience in supporting local women in Rwanda, Liberia, Burundi, Kosovo, Guatemala, and Timor-Leste, I knew that support to women affected by conflict and in countries undergoing transition could not wait. Ensuring gender equality in Afghanistan's legislative, judicial, and policy frameworks was an essential starting point for building the new future. I immediately prepared to visit Afghanistan with my team to identify and work with women on the ground who wanted change. We held intensive consultations with the government and local women with varied backgrounds—from doctors, teachers, and lawyers to displaced women and girls in the refugee camps.

I had established a local office in Kabul soon after the fall of the Taliban, and my regional office in South Asia, headed by Chandni Joshi, worked closely with the Ministry of Women's Affairs to build its capacity and support women in the provinces through the establishment of women development centres.

These centres fulfilled an urgent need at that time for safe spaces for women to meet, discuss their priorities, and gain access to social services. In partnership with local NGOs, doctors, and educators, the centres provided a range of services—healthcare, education, income, childcare, computer, and skills training and legal and psychological support. These centres also enhanced communication between local women's groups, local authorities, and the ministry.

By the time the first International Women's Day was celebrated in the country on 8 March 2002, the Ministry of Women's Affairs, headed by an exceptional leader, Sima Samar, and UNIFEM were able to mobilize over 1,000 Afghan women from seven districts to make their voices and demands heard. Representatives from various women's groups listed their demands after Minister Samar and I used our official address to put women's faces to the struggle for peace and security, supporting women's centrality to reconstruction and reforming the constitution, policies, and resources that supported development. The women who spoke after us highlighted the bitter reality that they had personally experienced and directed their demands for education, healthcare, employment, and equal citizenship to those with power and resources to make a difference. At the ruins of a Kabul cinema burnt down by the Taliban, Chairman Hamid Karzai and members of his cabinet, SRSG Brahimi, and Mary Robinson, the UN High Commissioner for Human Rights, listened to the aspirations of women from rural and urban areas and from all ethnic groups. Their message was united and clear—the women of Afghanistan wanted to help build a government accountable to all Afghans, at peace with itself and with its neighbours. They knew the cost of accumulated conflicts, what it meant to have sons, brothers, and husbands who were forced to fight, and daughters, forced to hide, totally excluded from public life.

These women were now the highest stakeholders of peace, stability, and development.

From that day, SRSG Brahimi became our champion and helped with UNIFEM's programmes and work to support 100 women leaders to engage with the 500-member Constitutional Loya Jirga (the Grand Assembly responsible for major decisions in Afghanistan) in December 2003. The work was intense, yet exciting. Together with Minister Samar, we organized networks of female lawyers and judges to engage with critical government leaders to promote the importance of empowering women. One innovative initiative was the engagement of constitutional legal expertise mobilized by Haifa Ghazaleh, director of the UNIFEM Office for Arab States. At that time, there was hope that the April 2003 roadmap of the Quartet—the UN, European Union, United States, and Russia—could achieve the final settlement of the Israeli–Palestinian conflict, and the creation of a Palestinian state based on the two-state solution. These male constitutional experts were now deployed to Afghanistan, and they worked consistently with the Afghan men attending the Loya Jirga on the value of equal citizenship rights. Eventually, after difficult negotiations, women were recognized as equal citizens for the first time in the constitution of Afghanistan.

The inclusion of women's equal rights in the constitution was a huge historic victory. However, societies do not erase discrimination overnight because of a new constitution. The legacy of discrimination remained entrenched and implementation was a big challenge. Many women shared their fears with me. In the southeast of the country, they saw threats from the resurgence of the Taliban. They saw new threats with the rise of the warlords again, supported by narco-trafficking that forms a large part of the economy. I asked them, 'Isn't it dangerous for you to be so engaged and so visible in your work?' Their answer was, 'Was it safer for us under the Taliban? Our daughters were deprived of education, we were confined to our homes, and severely punished in public when we broke their rules. We don't have a choice. We want a new future with this constitution.'

Equal citizenship for women in the constitution is real progress and will always be the beacon of hope for women in the country. However, today, the progress of women in Afghanistan is again at risk. Peace talks are taking place between the Taliban and the United States, the latter seeking to exit its longest military engagement. The talks focus on a ceasefire, withdrawal of foreign troops, and counter-terrorism assurances by the Taliban, but do not seriously include the voices and concerns of women. While women do want peace, they have voiced strong objections about the nature of peace being negotiated without them. With equal citizenship, over 3.5 million girls are now attending primary and secondary school; 100,000 women are in universities; and, in the 2018 parliamentary elections, over 400 female candidates ran for office. There is a deep fear that the return of the Taliban would threaten women's rights to education, employment, freedom of movement, and political participation. The international community has the obligation to ensure that the gains of Afghan women are not sacrificed in the name of 'peace'. After two decades of struggle, Afghan women are now empowered and demanding nothing less than inclusion and equality.

Supporting Women's Leadership for Sustainable Peace

Our work on rebuilding conflict-affected countries through supporting women's leadership, using the legitimacy of the SCR 1325, continued to deliver results. Some months after its passage, in October 2000, I appointed Ellen Johnson Sirleaf, former finance minister of Liberia, and Elizabeth Rehn, the first female defence minister of Finland and in the world, to lead the assessment on women, war and peace agenda that I had raised with the Security Council. When I first approached Ellen, her response was, 'Why me? I am not a feminist.' I replied, 'I need a finance minister who understands women's concerns in the reconstructing and financing of development in conflict-affected countries and who understands the world of politics, someone who has experience with the World Bank and financial institutions. There is no person better than you.' Ellen finally agreed and together with Elizabeth Rehn, we supported them to engage with women and political leaders in fourteen conflict zones, like the Democratic Republic of the Congo, Liberia, Somalia, Sierra Leone, Bosnia and Herzegovina, Colombia, and several refugee camps. Their assessment was completed in 2002 and Ellen became even more convinced of the importance of supporting and investing in women as a force for peace and reconstruction. Towards the end of 2003, at one of our strategic planning meetings, my regional director for western Africa, Florence Butega, who worked for many years in Liberia to support women's organizations in peacebuilding, alerted me that Ellen was contesting as a presidential candidate in the 2005 elections. It was time, she said, for us to organize a big women's conference on leadership and the future of the country. I agreed, and, in 2004, we organized the biggest conference on women, governance, and leadership in Liberia. We saw this as a great opportunity to support women's leadership from the ground up and worked closely with Women Affairs Minister Vabah Gayflor to educate women about the challenges and opportunities in post-conflict reconstruction and the importance of their vote. She later paid tribute to UNIFEM's long partnership with Liberian women, saying, 'They stood with us when we were mobilizing to support women's candidacy and leadership in the parliamentary and presidential elections.' The country and its women elected

Ellen Johnson Sirleaf as the first female President of Liberia and of Africa in January 2006. I attended the inauguration and watched the women dance in celebration.

UNIFEM already had a history of supporting women to become elected leaders through our African Women in Crisis Countries (AFWIC) programme , which was headed by Laketch Dirasse, my regional director for East, Central, and the Horn of Africa. Our work in Rwanda contributed to its highest percentage of women in parliament in the whole world, with women playing a bigger role to shape the new direction of their conflict-affected country. In July 2002, I was invited by the government of Rwanda to support women's role in the country's transition from post-conflict reconstruction to development. During our meeting, President Paul Kagame requested UNIFEM's support for women's entrepreneurship and training in new information technology to empower them to participate fully in economic life across all sectors and throughout all levels of economic activity. He saw this as essential to build strong economies, establish more stable and just societies, and quickly reduce women's poverty.

The importance of restorative justice, addressing the violence used against women, and of women in shaping the justice frameworks and rule-of-law institutions were highlighted to me in Timor-Leste. When I visited the country in 2002, I met Olga da Silva, a rural woman leader from the village of Mauxiga. She had learned about the Commission for Reception, Truth, and Reconciliation in Dili. Hearings were being held but her village was totally forgotten, even though they were the stronghold of resistance during the struggle for independence in which women were brutally attacked. She hitched a ride to Dili where she insisted to be a witness, telling her own story and that of her village. She said to me, 'No one came to this village after independence— not a single government minister, not a single UN person. We were totally forgotten in times of peace.' I wanted her to know that I was in the village that day because I celebrated her courage and leadership, and heard her voice all the way in New York, thanks to my national programme officer Melina Pires. Much of my time would be spent engaging with President Xanana Gusmão, Nobel Peace Laureate Bishop Carlos Filipe Ximenes Belo, women leaders, and parliament on the urgency of including women's perspectives at the heart of their justice, rule of law, and security sector reforms. And that is why I undertook the mission to Mauxiga with my local UNIFEM team, several other UN staff, and my daughter Lilianne.

The journey to her village seemed endless, as we meandered along the high precipice. As the day darkened, the fog grew thicker, covering our tracks. We were received with the greatest ceremonial honour with men on decorated horses and women from surrounding villages who had walked for miles in their traditional dresses. They greeted us with a traditional ceremony, dancing, and delicious local food. Despite the celebration, I saw that most people, men and women, were 'walking battlefields' in the sense that they still had battle wounds on their bodies. The deputy minister of health was with us and he made a commitment that there would be a clinic in the village. But they needed doctors. I immediately contacted my friends in the medical field in Singapore. A team of doctors, led by Dr Kanwaljit Soin, and supported by the Ministry of Foreign Affairs, responded positively. Later, the UN Department of Peacekeeping Operations told me that the women leaders in the villages were so grateful because they could not believe that their demands were heard and visiting officials would keep their promise. Timor-Leste taught me that the weaving of trust—between the local community and the government and the local community with the international system, knowing that people truly care and promises are kept—is the only way in which there will be trust in the multilateral system and its international norms and standards.

Soon after my visit to Timor-Leste, Palestinian and Israeli women leaders, Palestinian minister Zahira Kamal and Noami Chazan, chair of the Israeli Knesset, jointly wrote an official letter to me, as the Executive Director of UNIFEM, to convene the International Women's Commission (IWC) for a just and sustainable Palestinian and Israeli peace based on international law, human rights, and equality. They were inspired by SCR 1325 and were determined never to give up the struggle for peace and human dignity to preserve the values that safeguarded our humanity especially when it is hardest. They wanted the IWC to bring together Palestinian, Israeli, and international women leaders with experience in diplomacy, civil society, and political negotiations to help build common approaches to political solutions, act as an advisory and lobbying group supporting mediation for peace and reconciliation, increase the participation and perspectives of women at the peace table, and strengthen the relationships and factors to foster peace in the local communities on both sides. They knew that the security of one depended on the other.

After several preparatory meetings in Israel, the West Bank, and Gaza, I chaired a meeting in Istanbul in 2005, bringing together Palestinian and Israeli women leaders, supported by international experts, to draft the Charter of the IWC and agreed principles of working for the creation of the IWC. With its establishment, the members were ambitious and pushed many boundaries, meeting with members of the Quartet, visiting the European Parliament, the US State Department, and members of the US Congress. We addressed the leaders of the Socialist International at their Summit in Greece, invited by Prime Minister George Papandreou. In addition, I arranged for an IWC delegation, including Hanan Ashrawi, the minister of higher education and research of the Palestinian Authority, to visit New York during the opening of the UN General Assembly, participate in a side event, and meet with foreign ministers and senior officials. The secretary general of the Arab League, Amr Moussa, met the group during this trip and endorsed our proposals. The Israeli Knesset endorsed SCR 1325 and Palestinian President Mahmoud Abbas issued a presidential decree in support of SCR 1325.

It was a time of hope. I appointed three women heads of state as honorary co-chairs: Tarja Halonen, President of Finland; Ellen Johnson Sirleaf, President of Liberia; and Helen Clark, a three-term Prime Minister of New Zealand. On 13 May 2006, the IWC was able to organize a major international conference in East Jerusalem called, 'A Place at the Table', which was attended by over 300 leaders, diplomats, and other participants. It came up with many ideas and commitments that we were able to share with the Foreign Minister of Israel, Tzipi Livni. Many Palestinian women cried, as it was for the first time that they had visited East Jerusalem after restrictions were imposed on Palestinian movement after the intifada.

Our success, however, was short-lived. There were forces larger than ourselves that destroyed what we had achieved. We witnessed the attacks by Hamas, the building of walls, further control over mobility, and harsh military solutions by Israel. We could not accomplish what we wanted. But we all learned to never give up. Both sides wanted their children to remember that they tried and say, 'They had courage. They could not finish the journey for us but they have created another road for peace.' These experiences in different conflict-affected countries are testimony to the fact that, against all odds, people are the most powerful agents of change. And when supported and empowered in the direction envisioned by the UN Charter, they can shape their destiny towards a future of greater freedom and dignity.

Renewal within the UN

Within the United Nations renewals also happened. But it needed leaders in the system who dared to push it to the edge and keep it responsive to the changing realities. One of most significant achievements has been the recognition of sexual violence as a tactic of war, deliberately deployed for terror, and used in genocidal campaigns. The issue is now a regular item on the Security Council agenda and several resolutions have been passed on this. In particular, SCR 1820 (in 2008), SCR 1888 (in 2009), SCR 1960 (in 2010), SCR 2106 (in 2013) and SCR 2242 (in 2015) have all focused on obligations to prevention and protection, especially in the area of sexual violence. That means sexual violence in war now demands security-military and political responses. It must be addressed in troop deployments and peacekeeping tactics, peace processes, and war crimes tribunals. In the words of US Ambassador Don Steinberg, a staunch supporter of the issue, '[We stopped] men forgiving men for crimes against women.' In addition, the position at the rank of an Under-Secretary-General on Sexual Violence in Conflict was established in 2009 and Margot Wallström, foreign minister of Sweden, was appointed as its first SRSG.

Today, the number of senior women leaders within the UN has been on the rise—from SRSGs and special envoys of the secretary general, to the first female commander of a peacekeeping mission, to more women in peacekeeping. UN Secretary General António Guterres is committed to 'transforming the balance of power' and 'putting women at the centre of conflict prevention, peacemaking, peacebuilding and mediation efforts'. One of his first priorities as secretary general was to bring more women into leadership positions and has, in fact, achieved gender parity at senior leadership level. In addition, women leaders from civil society are regularly consulted by the Security Council on the women, peace, and security agenda and seen as movers of this agenda. This was very different from the first time when we brought women civil society to share their experiences with Security Council members using the Arria Formula. At that time, I was questioned by the chef de cabinet of the United Nations because some bureaucratic 'women focal points' complained that I had broken UN rules and participated in the Arria Formula. Luckily, I was forewarned about the two phone calls I would be receiving from him and was advised to avoid the word 'participate' but to say, 'I introduced the issue and the women leaders from civil society.' My team and I had become used to these 'turf wars', including some calling UNIFEM a 'deviant UN organization' for working so closely with civil society—a way of operating that some thought was 'too radical'. I drew courage from the many women leaders and men in the UN before me who brought transformation to the bureaucracy by knowing how to work productively with 'the third UN'[19] and so firmly stood my ground responding that we were becoming 'the UN of the future'.

To move the agenda forward, I was determined not to let any turf tensions dominate the relationships at UN headquarters. This meant identifying the areas where we could collaborate and others where we just needed to continue pushing the boundaries of

---

[19]   The first UN refers to member states, the second UN to the international UN civil service, and the third UN refers to supportive civil society, private sector, and academia.

institutional comfort to respond to urgent needs on the ground. This approach helped to develop a huge constituency determined to ensure the implementation of SCR 1325 and its monitoring by the Security Council, including through commemorating its anniversary every year in October. At the first celebration, I was told that Security Council resolutions do not have anniversaries. It was a break with tradition that has now become an institutional practice.

Another institutional break was to value the contribution of female peacebuilders and women who were at the front lines. Till that time, few women were recognized as Nobel Peace laureates and we wanted the UN to change this. I decided to establish the Millennium Peace Prize for Women on 8 March 2001—the first International Women's Day of the new millennium after the adoption of SCR 1325. This prize was to highlight the importance of women's leadership in peacebuilding and showcase the stories and commitments of women at the forefront of peace efforts, building trust across fractured communities. Our ceremony, in partnership with International Alert and supported by the USA UNIFEM National Committee, was held at the United Nations. The star-studded dinner at the UN Delegates Dining Room was sponsored and prepared by ten top chefs from New York City, led by chef Lidia Bastianich, and had the theme, 'Recipes for Peace'. The awardees were individuals and organizations—Flora Brovina from Kosovo, Asma Jahangir from Pakistan, Veneranda Nzambazamariya from Rwanda, Women in Black (International), Ruta Pacifica de las Mujeres (Colombia), and Leitana Nehan Women's Development Agency (Papua New Guinea). It was an unforgettable evening. But, what was most unforgettable for me was the conversation with the awardees, a few months later, when they described how their awards and the international recognition they received from the UN served as protective shields for them back home, as they continued with their difficult and often politically dangerous work.

In the field, change happened immediately with SRSG Brahimi when he was put in charge of Iraq. He took the initiative to request meetings with local women leaders. Similarly, SRSG Sérgio de Mello worked with UNIFEM to organize the largest national women's consultation in Iraq when he took over. His plans were derailed by a violent tragedy. A few days before the conference, on 19 August 2003, the UN office in Baghdad was attacked by a suicide bomber, driving a truck into the building. The bomb killed SRSG de Mello and twenty-two other UN staff members. This was one of the darkest days I had experienced during my time with the UN.

As I write, our world is far from peaceful. New conflicts have emerged, such as those in Syria and Yemen, and many old ones, such as those in the Democratic Republic of the Congo, have continued. The insights gained from the struggle for SCR 1325 and its implementation are more relevant than ever, not only for women but also for all who face discrimination and denial of basic human rights. While we have yet to find an end to many conflicts and forms of violence, there have been some remarkable successes as well, although often not widely known. One such success was Colombia, where SCR 1325 was a critical tool for the women's movement to facilitate the participation of women at the negotiating table during the 2016 peace process. Women leaders from Norway and Sweden informed me of their role in this at the Women Mediators Network Meeting in Oslo in March 2018, which I attended. In Asia, during its thirty-first summit in 2017, the leaders of the ASEAN formally adopted the women, peace, and security agenda, which I am supporting in my new capacity as a member of the UN Secretary General António Guterres's High-Level Advisory Board on Mediation.

Conclusion

The journey of SCR 1325 taught me some of the most critical and hardest lessons of my entire career at the UN. I learned that although the UN was founded on principles of peace and human rights, principles are not enough in a world where the politics of hatred, division, violence, and exclusion permeates many of our societies. Working on these many situations of conflict, I learned that we must be attentive to the reality that many powerful actors hold values that go against those enshrined in the UN Charter, and that often these actors mobilize popular fear to fuel a politics of division and hatred. I realized that principles and norms of the UN must be continuously renewed and reaffirmed, especially when they are shaken in the face of violence that dehumanizes others, shatters the moral compass of entire societies, and unleashes a downward spiral of revenge. I learnt that particularly when lives are at stake and political leadership is critical, then those who want to create change within a system as complex as the UN must engage leadership at multiple levels, linking realities on the ground to high levels of decision-making.

Through my work on SCR 1325, I also learned that space for change must be created and leaders of change must be legitimized. But for change to last, it cannot simply be imposed from the top-down; rather, it must be championed by leaders who come from within communities themselves, deployed as a force to mobilize participation in transition and recovery for all members of the society. I learnt that there is an important role for a strengthened multilateral system, but that the international community also cannot be expected to fix all problems, especially at a time when the system itself is plagued by the politics of shifting balance of power globally. Thus, we cannot depend on the UN and member states alone; we must identify, recognize, legitimize, and invest in leadership and agency for change at all levels on the basis of shared global values and responsibility. The UN remains an indispensable global institution in ensuring peace, security, and equality. But without vision, courage, and people willing to take the risk to make those norms reality, it will not be fit for purpose to serve its constituency. Indeed, it is 'We, the Peoples' who make the UN the great institution that it can be.

8

Taking Leadership in Asia-Pacific

'It always seems impossible until it's done.'

—*Nelson Mandela*

One July evening in New York, my phone rang. It was one of those evenings in 2007 when I was reflecting on my proudest period in UNIFEM—working on the women, peace, and security agenda—and my deep disappointment that no matter how much work we did or how we grew, UNIFEM was still not afforded the institutional status of other UN organizations to more effectively fulfil our mandate. I stirred from my thoughts and picked up the phone. The UN Secretary General Ban Ki-moon was calling from San Francisco where he had just landed to attend a ceremony to commemorate the 1945 signing of the UN Charter in the city. He wanted to personally convey that he had just appointed me the United Nations Under-Secretary-General and the first woman to head Economic and Social Commission for Asia and the Pacific ESCAP. He requested me to report almost immediately for duty. I thanked Mr Ban for his trust and assured him that I would perform my duties to the best of my abilities. I was excited to be returning to Asia.

The whole process of recruitment was highly confidential and no one in UNIFEM knew about the possibility of my leaving the organization. The announcement was to be made at noon the next day. I called Joanne to inform her and together we organized a staff meeting early the next morning. My staff was in a state of shock. It was a difficult time to be leaving UNIFEM. Despite all our successes, the organization was once again under threat of being integrated into UNDP. Under the 2006 UN reform initiative, there were already discussions of merging the larger entities like UNFPA and UNICEF with UNDP to form a consolidated UN Development entity. There was strong resistance from the powerful heads of these entities; tensions were high and the merger efforts had stalled. The then minister for development cooperation of the Netherlands, Agnes van Ardenne, became impatient and ordered a suspension of some budget allocation to UNDP core resources unless it could show its strength by integrating smaller organizations over which it had some control. She suggested UNIFEM. Despite my meetings with her, she went ahead with her recommendation and made it extremely difficult for both UNIFEM and UNDP. Joanne was one of the first to observe that the 'gender architecture' of the UN system broken by turf wars needed a large-scale overhaul. We decided that we should use the UN reform to initiate this and to stop UNIFEM's integration into UNDP.

The seeds of what became UN Women—the merger of four UN entities for gender equality, including UNIFEM—were sown. There were four separate UN organizations, with different mandates, focused on gender equality. UNIFEM was by far the largest of the four, with extensive programmes and ground presence. Several supporters advised me to take the path of UNFPA and be fully, independent as it was historically also administered by UNDP. This was, in fact, one of the recommendations made by the study we had commissioned under the auspices of the UNIFEM Consultative Committee chaired from 2004 to 2007 by Prince Zeid Ra'ad al-Hussein, ambassador of Jordan to the United Nations. Led by Nafis Sadik, former executive director of the UNFPA, the study sought to use the 2006 UN reform agenda to review the existing UN's gender architecture and recommend future scenarios for UNIFEM. The study recommended three other scenarios for the gender architecture: follow the route of UNAIDs, become an entity like the Office of the High Commissioner of Human Rights, or merge the existing gender entities. Of course, our preference was to have a fully independent UNIFEM. However, I knew that this possibility could not succeed given the pressures of UN reform, the turf wars among the fragmented gender entities, the ambition of UNFPA to expand its gender mandate, and the changes in political environment of donor countries. There was no appetite among member states to support the creation of a separate UN organization without some kind of merger.

After intense discussions within UNIFEM and our Consultative Committee, we agreed that consolidation was a shorter route to a more powerful UN institution for women's empowerment. My staff began mobilizing our constituency to support this, aware that this entity would be building on the strong foundations of UNIFEM. We were able to mobilize over a million signatures of support, which local women leaders delivered to the three co-chairs of the High-Level Panel on UN System-wide Coherence. Along with a growing global civil society network of women's rights organizations led by the Gender Equality Architecture (GEAR) campaign, we seized the opportunity of the UN reform agenda to push for an Under-Secretary-General post for a new 'joined-up' UN organization for women's rights that would bring the normative and operational mandates of the four existing gender equality organizations to create the UN Entity for Gender Equality and the Empowerment of Women.

While there was support from several member states for the idea, resistance was very strong from the gender entities and UNDP. They saw this as UNIFEM's initiative and ambitious 'takeover'. While I wanted to see things through, my new duties as UN Under-Secretary-General and in ESCAP could wait no longer; the fight would have to be left to Joanne and my team. They continued to use 'inside-outside' partnerships, working with member states and mobilizing women constituencies globally. Today, UN Women, formed through the successful merger in 2010, is regarded as the 'poster child' of the 2006 UN Reform agenda with a seat at the highest level of UN decision-making and the ending of turf wars among gender entities.

As I prepared to take over the leadership of ESCAP, I was humbled by the trust of the Secretary-General and the senior management of the UN in my ability to renew complex institutions. I knew the history of ESCAP, the important role it played in the policy directions of post-war Asia, and how so many people have worked to reform the institution through better leadership when the institution and values of the UN were betrayed. I was determined to use my leadership and the institutional status of an Under-Secretary-General to bring excellence back to ESCAP, increase its relevance, and make it a trusted UN partner in the Asia-Pacific region.

At the personal level, returning to Asia was a gift I will always treasure. It allowed me to bring my scattered family together after enduring over 13 years of a long-distance relationship with Yew Teng. Pauline had returned to Malaysia to join him in 2001 after she graduated magna cum laude and received a presidential award for excellence from New York University. Lilianne decided to stay with me after the September 11 terrorist attack in Lower Manhattan and continued with her masters at Columbia University in New York. After graduating with distinction and receiving a scholarship by Oxford University to do a PhD, she left for the United Kingdom, but decided to give it all up to work as the Oxfam coordinator in Aceh when the 2004 tsunami devastated the Indonesian province. While I marvelled at how our daughters had managed themselves so wonderfully, I was determined to create a beautiful base for the family to come together and enjoy each other again. Returning to Bangkok allowed this to happen.

There was also a promise to keep. As I was preparing to return to Cambridge in 1975, Grandma pulled me aside as we said our goodbyes. There were tears in her eyes as she told me that my mother's last words to her were, 'Take care of my children.' She felt that she would not see me again and had one request. Her children, my aunt and uncle, had no family of their own as they remained single and the child from a disadvantaged background that the family had adopted was limited in abilities. She stressed that I was all the family had and treasured. She looked me in the eyes and said, 'Take care of my children.' This was the promise I made to her. I had tried my best to keep it by visiting them with my children as often as I could and spent nearly every Christmas with them. Returning to the region would allow me to take better care of them as they grew older.

A few weeks after our staff meeting, I returned to Asia. The region was struggling with multiple threats to its development, from natural disasters and climate change to the global financial and economic crisis that struck in 2008. It was time to immerse myself again in the opportunities and challenges of the Asia-Pacific region with its changing development landscape. As a more mature and senior UN leader, I had the authority to reposition the UN Regional Commission and help build regional cooperation for inclusive and sustainable development. My challenge was how to exercise the kind of leadership that could reform ESCAP to be a trusted UN platform that could thrive in the dynamic region, rethinking new drivers of growth for Asia-Pacific's next transition towards sustainable and shared prosperity. This was not an easy task.

Despite having structures and formal authority that came with its long history, ESCAP had lost much of its early dynamism by the eighties. When my appointment was announced, there was an op-ed piece in the *Bangkok Post* on 16 December 2007, saying that ESCAP was seen by many as 'a moribund institution' and hoped that I could revive it. The challenge was to give the organization strong purpose and direction again, and I was determined to succeed. My first few months were spent understanding the internal and external dynamics by listening to the staff identifying their 'building blocks and stumbling blocks' and communicating my vision and expectations. I engaged member states and encouraged them to seriously use ESCAP as their platform to address development challenges facing the region. I mobilized some of the best people in the region to provide intellectual resources and advice and built shared understanding of our mission and strategy among the staff as well as developed their capacity when there was an initial skills gap. I worked hard to win the confidence of senior decision-makers, and put together a team to provide member states with the best ideas, rigorous analysis, and networks of knowledge so that ESCAP could be a valued platform where Asia-Pacific leaders could convene to discuss and seek common understanding and regional solutions. This often meant being proactive and taking risks to turn the various crises in the region into opportunities to advance together towards a more resilient Asia-Pacific founded on shared prosperity, social equity, and sustainability.

A Cyclone like No Other

In 2007, at the time of my appointment, Myanmar hit the headlines because of the protests led by Burmese monks, triggered by the military government's removal of fuel subsidies. In the first week in office, I realized that this was one member state in a very difficult situation and that this political situation would make it almost impossible to engage with it on the economic and social agenda. But then, on the 2 May 2008, Cyclone Nargis struck Myanmar, causing widespread destruction and devastation across the Ayeyarwady Delta. I was in Jakarta on 8 May at a meeting with Bill Gates on information technology for inclusive and sustainable development when I received news that the numbers of those who had died or were missing had reached 100,000. The cyclone was the deadliest ever recorded in the North Indian Ocean basin and the second deadliest named tropical storm of all time. It left more than 140,000 people dead or missing and more than 800,000 homeless, with an estimated 2.4 million people—one-third of the entire population of Ayeyarwady and Yangon divisions—affected by the disaster. The cyclone devastated farming and fishing communities, destroying over 700,000 homes and causing severe damage to critical infrastructure, including the destruction of schools and three-quarters of the hospitals and clinics in the area. The damage was estimated at $4 billion.

Myanmar's relationship with many Western countries had been tense for about two decades before the cyclone struck, and the government made it clear that they did not want outside help. The presence of a United States naval ship and a French warship created great suspicion from Myanmar as to the nature of international humanitarian intervention, particularly as there was a talk around invoking the UN principle of 'Responsibility to Protect'. Pressure continued to mount from the international community, with some diplomats calling for life-saving assistance to be delivered without the consent of the government. What crossed my mind was how isolated the country had become, that although there was a complete lack of trust towards the outside world that had to be bridged, the outside world also had no idea how best to engage. Many people worked behind the scenes to find solutions that could work. As executive secretary of ESCAP, I felt, like many others, that ASEAN and the UN could together play an even stronger role to build trust and facilitate humanitarian cooperation.

Singapore was the chair of ASEAN when Cyclone Nargis struck. At the emergency meeting of ASEAN foreign ministers in Singapore, George Yeo, of Singapore, and Hassan Wirajuda, of Indonesia, persuaded the group to allow ASEAN take a leading role in the humanitarian response. ASEAN's collective response to Nargis was confirmed on 19 May. The decision was immediately conveyed to the UN Secretary General Ban Ki-moon and led to the ASEAN–UN cooperation that followed. I accompanied the secretary general to the ASEAN–UN International Pledging Conference on 25 May in Yangon, chaired by Singapore's foreign minister, George Yeo. It was the first visit by a UN secretary general since the 1970s. Mr Ban was able to get full humanitarian access for the international community after his meeting with Senior General Than Shwe. It was a real breakthrough that took everyone by surprise, and one that helped achieve some early successes. They agreed to a two-tiered structure with a mandate to manage humanitarian access. The ASEAN Humanitarian Task Force (AHTF) functioned as the diplomatic and policy-level body of the ten ASEAN countries and a Yangon-based Tripartite Core Group (TCG) was established to oversee the everyday operations of the relief and recovery efforts. I was pleased to be appointed to the AHTF's Advisory Group, assisting them to make policy decisions and establish the priorities and targets with regard to the implementation of the ASEAN-led initiative.

It started my close collaboration and friendship with Dr Surin Pitsuwan, the secretary general of ASEAN. Together, we visited the communities and people affected by Cyclone Nargis to fully capture the realities on the ground and guide recovery efforts. We paid special attention to the humanitarian needs of women and children and the rebuilding of livelihoods, homes, schools, and healthcare centres. The AHTF and the TCG facilitated the formulation of the Post-Nargis Joint Assessment (PONJA), which provided the comprehensive understanding of the damage and loss, and the resources needed for post-disaster relief and reconstruction. This was accompanied by the Post-Nargis Recovery and Preparedness Plan (PONREPP), which set out a three-year recovery strategy running from 2009 to 2011. However, the economic sanctions against Myanmar created a complicated backdrop for donors who struggled to fund the activities beyond the immediate relief efforts. Despite this initial reluctance among donors, I co-chaired a donor conference at ESCAP with Dr Surin on 25 November 2009, and, together, we succeeded to raise 90 per cent of the requested $103 million urgently needed by the affected communities in the delta as identified by the PONREPP.

In addition, Myanmar's Deputy Foreign Minister U Kyaw Thu, as the Chair of the TCG, Dr Surin, and I worked together to explore good practices and lessons learnt from the region of how governments successfully managed complex post-disaster reconstruction efforts. This helped Myanmar with knowledge and guiding principles in preparing the recovery plans. Our collaboration culminated in the ESCAP–ASEAN Regional High-level Expert Group meeting on Post-Nargis recovery in October 2008. We convened more than 100 regional experts and high-ranking decision-makers from governments, international partners, the World Bank, the ADB, and UN agencies with interest in Myanmar. Much of the discussions guided the preparation of the PONREPP. Deputy Minister U Kyaw Thu found that the experience 'went beyond all expectations' and requested that I explore possibilities to work beyond the cyclone-affected areas to support the longer-term economic and social development of Myanmar.

I had already made several visits to Myanmar and would meet regularly with then Prime Minister Thein Sein and his team of reformist generals. We had many productive conversations, especially when he had just returned from the Nargis-affected communities. In one conversation, he opened up about the concerns of the local people he had met and their lack of appreciation. We had an interesting discussion on the difference between human security and military security. I stressed that the country had been traumatized by the cyclone. People were anxious and wanted to know how his leadership was going 'to build back better'. I shared how it was not enough to show military power through the mobilization to provide humanitarian relief alone. It was important to lay the foundations for better healthcare, education, housing, and livelihood opportunities to ensure that people have a greater sense of security. I was aware that people had experienced the use of military force in land confiscation, environmental degradation, and population displacement, especially associated with the building of major dams or in the management of natural resources like jade and timber. Without mentioning this, I stressed the importance of rebuilding social trust by prioritizing the development needs of local communities.

Soon after, the government requested me to form a development partnership with them at a very tense time. It was a difficult tightrope to walk because Myanmar was politically isolated. The West was strongly opposed to the country's human rights record. The UN secretary general's good offices were rightly focused on securing the release of political prisoners—especially Aung San Suu Kyi—and the overall human rights and governance situation. The UN Resident Coordinator, Charles Petrie, had been asked to leave the country for raising concerns about poverty conditions following the monks' uprising. Yet, the ESCAP mandate of supporting economic and social development in all our member states gave us reason to stay engaged and, if possible, find new areas of rebuilding trust and cooperation. I decided to push as hard as I could on the development front, even when the politics left much to be desired, opening the new chapter for engagement and using the newly forged economic and social space to further the dialogue that put people and poverty reduction at the centre of the development agenda.

Permission was granted for me to visit rural areas of the dry zone and give feedback. I highlighted economic and food–water insecurity; that many children, especially girls, were not in schools, families were struggling, and people were migrating as cheap labour to neighbouring countries. I suggested and succeeded in bringing in some top minds to discuss economic and social issues, especially rural development. The result was the Second Development Partnership Forum that allowed practitioners and eminent international scholars, such as Nobel Laureate for Economics Joseph Stiglitz and local researchers and experts like Dr U Myint, a friend of Aung San Suu Kyi, to exchange experiences and ideas with government leaders and civil society in the presence of the diplomatic corps. President Thein Sein referred to it as helping to provide the initial direction and substance to his economic reform agenda when it was most needed. In his inaugural address as President, he talked about the struggle against poverty, 'clean governance', and the need to close the development gaps in the country. The risk I took has been regarded by many as helping to catalyse the promise of development in the early opening up of the country from its former isolation. Personally, I knew that it would be a very long struggle for the government to engage, build trust, and improve the lives of marginalized communities.

However, my action also showed how ESCAP could be a relevant platform and convener, and how the UN could use its regional assets in seemingly intractable circumstances.

New Script for an Inclusive and Sustainable Asia-Pacific

The dynamism of Asia and the Pacific had been well-documented by the time I took the leadership of ESCAP. In the thirty years between 1980 and 2010, developing Asia's real gross domestic product (GDP) grew at an annual average rate of slightly over 7 per cent, compared to the global average of 2.8 per cent. As a result, the per capita income of Asia rose five-fold during this period, while the global per capita income increased by just one and a half times. Asia's rapid growth was supported by a favourable external economic environment and opportunities arising from globalization. However, the global economic environment had changed dramatically with the onset of the financial crisis in 2008. It was now clear that, burdened by huge debt and global imbalances, the advanced economies of the West were no longer able to play the role of engines of growth for the Asia-Pacific region which they played in the past. Sustaining growth in the future would require rebalancing the Asia-Pacific economies in favour of more domestic and regional sources of demand.

Member states were concerned with the downside risks and policy challenges that the region faced in sustaining its dynamism. Their fundamental challenge was to find alternative engines for sustaining growth in the aftermath of the financial crisis, close development gaps, and address persistent poverty and hunger. Despite drastic reductions in the levels of poverty, income inequalities had risen significantly within countries and among countries in different subregions. Even during the Asian boom years, impressive growth figures of the gross domestic product masked serious economic and social inequalities in terms of income and education, as well as lack of access to basic services like drinking water, sanitation, healthcare and electricity. Nearly one billion people worked in poorly paid jobs with no social protection. These dimensions of development were inadequately addressed in countries, especially in South Asia, with entrenched rural–urban, class, caste, gender, and ethnic divides. I saw how, even in the emerging economies of South East Asia, the creation of decent and productive jobs remained a key challenge. In these richer economies, wages remained the most important source of income for most people, but millions worked in vulnerable employment characterized by poor labour and safety standards as low-waged or undocumented migrants. Without social protection for people in Asia, multiple forms of deprivation tended to overlap and reinforce each other, undermining the social fabric and deepening a sense of injustice.

In addition, the region was suffering from a mounting ecological burden and vulnerability to climate change and natural disasters. For many of our Pacific Island states, these were looming questions of their survival or extinction. During my term, I visited several Pacific Island states with UN Secretary General Ban Ki-moon. Our 2011 visit to Kiribati and the meetings with local villages, including children, best captured the fears of being submerged and concerns with the effects of climate change on their low-lying islands. As we watched the rising sea levels at high tide, we witnessed the serious threats impacting the livelihood and security of people as the sea inundated the villages, the fields with their crops, and the roads of Tarawa, the capital of Kiribati. We could no longer grow first and clean up later. I seized these multiple threats as opportunities to bring together key decision-makers and influential thinkers to rethink our development strategy, write a new script, and create a new development paradigm in navigating the rapidly changing development landscape of the twenty-first century. Together, we framed the debates on how best to reinvest in ourselves; maintain the region's dynamism; address the existing economic, social, and ecological imbalances in the region; and facilitate Asia-Pacific's next transformation towards a more inclusive and sustainable future.

It was a historic opportunity to help the region sustain its dynamism by placing people and the planet at the centre of its policy agenda. As the UN's intergovernmental platform for decision-making in the region, ESCAP could use its convening authority to bring together member states and support them with rigorous economic–social analysis and technical assistance. I established a distinguished lecture series delivered by eminent figures, including three Nobel Laureates of Economics—Amartya Sen, Joseph Stiglitz, and Robert Mundell. They engaged, through public lectures and closed door meetings, with prime ministers and cabinet ministers, and held roundtable discussions with ambassadors, public policy officials, and senior ESCAP staff. Throughout, they showed how developmental challenges such as poverty and widespread disparities in social and physical infrastructure could be turned into opportunities for sustaining future growth and dynamism. Our 'bottom billion', if lifted out of poverty and allowed to join the mainstream of the region's consumers, could help sustain growth in Asia and the Pacific for decades to come. This, however, required faster progress towards closing the development gaps through broad-based investments in education, healthcare services, social protection, and basic infrastructure. All of these measures could facilitate access to employment and business opportunities for all social groups besides generating new aggregate demand to sustain growth and inclusive development.

Turning Crises into Opportunities

While helping the region deal with the global economic headwinds, I did not anticipate a major governance crisis that erupted right in front of me, soon after I took office. Thailand was caught in a full-blown national crisis around corruption and to bring down the government. It was the biggest political battle between 'the red shirts and the yellow shirts'—the supporters of former Prime Minister Thaksin and the royalist middle-class elite. The gates of ESCAP were blocked and the main access road to the UN building was occupied for months by political demonstrators. Violence had broken out and Bangkok was on fire. As the Under-Secretary-General of the United Nations, I was responsible for the security and safety of the UN system, staff, and their families in Thailand during the intense political struggle and gun violence that erupted regularly over my tenure at ESCAP. Working closely with my security team, I provided security updates, arranged for the staff to work from home when necessary, and supervised the travel of the staff whenever 'yellow shirt protestors' from the People's Alliance for Democracy occupied and shut down the Suvarnabhumi Airport—Thailand's main international airport and major transit hub for the region—blocking the gateway to the country.

Our work continued in the 'new normal' of political chaos. Thailand took over as the chair of ASEAN and organized the ASEAN summit on 11 April 2009 at the Royal Cliff Beach Resort Hotel in Pattaya. Prime Minister Abhisit Vejjajiva invited the UN secretary general and personally persuaded him to come. As I waited for the arrival of Secretary General Ban Ki-moon, my phone rang. ASEAN Secretary General Surin Pitsuwan had called, requesting me to urgently stop the secretary general from landing at the U-Tapao Airport. The storming of the ASEAN summit venue had just happened. The red shirt protestors had broken through police barricades and forced their way into the hotel after breaking through the glass doors. This forced the shutting down of the summit and the emergency evacuation of ASEAN heads of state by boats and airlifted from the rooftop by helicopters. I immediately called the UN secretary general who was en route to Thailand, conveyed the seriousness of the situation, and arranged for his arrival at the Suvarnabhumi Airport. That evening, I arranged for Dr Surin to brief Mr Ban Ki-moon by phone as I prepared for his safe return to New York. It was a huge embarrassment for the Royal Government of Thailand and the prime minister, as reports of the ASEAN Summit being stormed by protestors and images of delegates escaping by helicopter captured headlines around the world.

ASEAN member states were very concerned and some even suggested that Vietnam should take over the chair of ASEAN in order to allow Thailand to sort out its political problems. Thailand refused. A few weeks later, I was invited to meet Foreign Minister Kasit Piromya over lunch. He informed me the ASEAN summit would be restaged in the royal town of Hua Hin at the end of October with a strong military presence. I was requested to be part of the team he was putting together to help with conceptualizing critical issues facing the region that could be addressed by the East Asian Summit. This would include the ten ASEAN member states and the dialogue partners from the Asia-Pacific region. I shared that in a region as diverse as the Asia-Pacific, capabilities and resources varied across countries, giving rise to complementarities and opportunities for mutually beneficial exchange, which could be unlocked by enhancing regional economic integration. Given the challenges and opportunities that the 2008 economic and financial crisis posed for the region, I suggested that we should focus on working with member states to identify major initiatives for regional cooperation. Eventually, we came up with the idea of regional connectivity, on which ESCAP would work with ASEAN and the ADB.

ESCAP had, over the years, facilitated connectivity through international agreements on the Asian Highway and the Trans-Asian Railway. I had an excellent team in the Transport Division of ESCAP and they were working on a new intergovernmental agreement on dry ports as part of our vision of an international, integrated, and intermodal transport and logistics system. I wanted them to go beyond this to focus on building sustainable infrastructure for the twenty-first century, and putting people back into discussions about transport and connectivity. This meant investing in renewable energy generation capacities and 'smart grids' to better share energy resources, improve efficiency, and promote a greater share for renewables and clean energy. It meant building connectivity through investments in regional railway networks and broadband ICT infrastructure. It meant promoting the 'software of connectivity', regulations to support people-to-people connectivity, and better market access of remote communities. Together with ADB President Haruhiko Kuroda, I was invited by Thailand as the chair of ASEAN to present these ideas on regional connectivity to the sixteen heads of state from East Asia, South Asia, ASEAN, and Australia attending the 2009 East Asian Summit, becoming the first UN official to address the summit.

Two years later, the Royal Government of Thailand changed to the 'Red Shirts' and Yingluck Shinawatra became the country's first female prime minister. The political divide continued and I was prepared for that. But, in October 2011, something unexpected happened. Thailand experienced its worst flood. The powerful storm affecting the country threatened to inundate Bangkok. Floodwaters were approaching from every direction.

There was an ocean surge from the south, reservoirs to the north of Bangkok were filled beyond capacity, the Bangkok canal system was overflowing, and the torrential rain continued to fall. The government faced the prospect of having to release water from reservoirs, trying to balance water levels to protect power systems, hospitals, communication networks, and other critical infrastructure for millions of people.

I called the prime minister's office to ask how the UN system could help. When I met the prime minister, she explained that while the government had significant political, technical, and financial capacity to deal with many aspects of the floods, it was lacking real-time satellite imagery data. This data would provide up-to-the-minute information on the inundations surrounding Bangkok to manage the release of water in ways that would protect people and infrastructure. I quickly convened a senior technical team of specialists within ESCAP and the UN system. In just over twenty-four hours, the team reached out to assemble a powerful network of spacefaring member states, including China, Japan, the Republic of Korea, and India, who contributed satellite data. Working with the regional satellite-based disaster information monitoring network, Sentinel Asia, and supported by a dozen world space agencies, the UN as a system enabled Thailand's Geo-Informatics and Space Technology Development Agency to access near real time flood data from the global constellation of earth observation satellites. This enabled Thailand to avoid releasing floodwaters into Bangkok, saving countless lives, millions of dollars in likely infrastructure damage, and the country's largest business centre.

From the time I took office, a string of severe natural disasters continuously besieged the region. Not only was there the worst cyclone in Myanmar and the worst flooding in Thailand, there were also disastrous floods in Pakistan and India; typhoons in

Philippines, Bangladesh, and the Pacific Islands; earthquakes in China; tsunamis in Japan and Indonesia; and droughts in the Russian Federation. Asia-Pacific is the world's hotspot for natural disasters, and disasters and climate change are the largest development threats for our region. ASEAN Secretary General Surin Pitsuwan and I worked closely and brought our teams together to focus on this agenda. It was eventually incorporated into the ASEAN–UN comprehensive partnership to provide a coordinated regional response to shared vulnerabilities. This was facilitated by President Susilo Bambang Yudhoyono of Indonesia when the country became the chair of ASEAN in 2011.

At the sixty-eighth ESCAP Commission Session in May 2012, the ESCAP study, 'Growing Together: Economic Integration for an Inclusive and Sustainable Asia-Pacific Century', proposed a four-pronged policy agenda as the new development script for the Asia-Pacific. Regional connectivity and the coordinated regional response to shared vulnerabilities became two of the building blocks for regional cooperation. The third was to build a broader, more integrated market in Asia and the Pacific to connect high-growth economies with landlocked, least developed countries and ocean economics of small island states to form 'corridors of prosperity', spreading the benefits of regional growth more widely. The region had already started discussing an important initiative to create a larger integrated market through the Regional Comprehensive Economic Partnership (RCEP), covering ASEAN+6 countries. Bringing together some of the largest and most dynamic economies of the world in a single grouping would provide the nucleus of an integrated regional market to which other countries could accede to in future. The final building block was further developing the regional financial architecture to better deploy the region's savings—including excess foreign exchange reserves and private savings—for productive purposes and close the gaps in the region's infrastructure.

The ESCAP Commission considered this four-pronged policy agenda as part of a long-term strategy to build the economic community of Asia and the Pacific to exploit the potential of regional economic integration and achieve a more resilient and sustainable region founded on shared prosperity and social equity.

Over fifty years ago, at a ministerial conference on regional economic cooperation convened by ESCAP, which was known as ECAFE then, the member states resolved to set up the Asian Development Bank to assist them in their pursuit of development as they were coming out of the yoke of colonialism. Half a century later, member states of ESCAP had, by means of a commission resolution, requested me, as the executive secretary of ESCAP, to convene a ministerial conference on regional economic integration in late 2013 to seriously consider the proposals made in the ESCAP study and take steps towards implementing them, as they faced the challenge of sustaining their dynamism in the wake of multiple threats and the global financial crisis. My leadership at ESCAP concentrated on assisting the region in moving ahead with this policy agenda. My team and I focused on building our institutional capacity to support countries to address development gaps and inequalities; promote green growth and the blue economy; facilitate trade, transport, and digital connectivity; and strengthen governance practices for the well-being of the people and planet. I remain encouraged by the standing ovation of member states at the end of my term, an indication that our multilateral institution had been revitalized for regional cooperation towards a more inclusive, sustainable, and resilient Asia Pacific.

Closing Reflections

Our world has changed again since I left ESCAP in 2014. We have entered a new era of uncertainty, anxiety, and complexity.

While our world is coming closer together through economic integration and mobile connection, it is simultaneously drifting further apart. Excessive inequality has marginalized people, damaged communities, and eroded trust between people and established political institutions and leaders. Our children's generation will be fully impacted by multiple disruptions from the Fourth Industrial Revolution, the climate emergency, and conflicts we do not know how to end. Multilateralism has been weakened when it is most needed for productive conversations to mobilize shared solutions to global problems and strengthen the universal values that bind us as a human community. As I write, the world is in turmoil, devastated by the coronavirus pandemic which has infected over eighty million people and killed over one and a half million globally. The social, economic, and health impacts of the pandemic are unprecedented and magnified the inequality, insecurity, and humanitarian challenges worldwide. Managing Covid-19 has forced borders to close, disrupted global supply chains, and destroyed industries and small businesses, creating joblessness on a scale not seen in peacetime. The world is in urgent need of global leadership and coordinated global responses to an unprecedented global emergency since World War II. It is precisely at times like this that the leadership and values of the multilateral system are needed to support those fighting the pandemic and those who can support global economic recovery, human security, and peacebuilding in the Covid-19 era.

As we enter this dangerous era of uncertainty and anxiety, a multilateralism that can deliver in the changing landscape of threats and opportunities is more needed than ever. The seventy-fifth anniversary of the UN, twenty-fifth anniversary of the FWCW, the twentieth anniversary of Security Council Resolution 1325 on women, peace and security started a process of global reflection and conversations initiated by the UN Secretary General António

Guterres. The results are striking. People on the ground want an effective people-centred multilateralism, pushing the system beyond its comfortable boundaries of interstate cooperation. In the words of the Secretary-General, 'People are thinking big— about transforming the global economy, accelerating the transition to zero carbon, ensuring universal health coverage, ending racial injustice and ensuring that decision-making is more open and inclusive.' He has requested his High-Level Advisory Board on Mediation, of which I am a member, to share our thoughts as he and the member states put in place 'the inclusive, networked and effective multilateralism' to address the overwhelming challenges of today and tomorrow.

At this pivotal moment of urgency, profound rethinking and transformation, what reflections can I share, based on my experience, about making multilateralism work in this era of great turbulence? How do we reshape power and leadership to restore the eroded trust between people who feel marginalized and established political institutions and leaders? How do we make the rule-based multilateral order relevant to regional and local realities? How do we open up spaces and new approaches for multilateral cooperation to address shared challenges?

My experience in the Asia-Pacific during the global financial crisis, political tensions, and natural disasters showed how the UN could use its regional assets and partnerships in seemingly intractable circumstances. From my time at ESCAP, the only way to convince doubters of our value and purpose was to make sure that ESCAP was a UN platform for action; that it delivered for the region and its people in some of the hardest times and strengthened regional cooperation when that was most vital. I showed in concrete situations that we knew how to build relationships of trust with member states, regional organizations, and networks that could mobilize knowledge and solutions to help deal with disruptions and headwinds. Independent of politics, I decided to always put vulnerable people first and show that we are tuned in to real needs and concerns of the region.

Regional cooperation based on the shared values and shared responsibilities, as enshrined in the UN Charter, can help address a crisis of the magnitude of Covid-19. Region by region, cooperation could help protect personal health and safety, especially of the most vulnerable. It could restore supply chains, support small and medium enterprises, and revive economies and livelihoods by strengthening coordination on regional trade, investment, transport, and digital connectivity. It could ensure that measures to stimulate the economy recognize women's work in the informal sector and their care work as highly valued in the formal economy and in the Covid-19 response and recovery. It could take better care of 'people on the move' such as low-waged migrants and refugees. Our post-Covid-19 world could eventually be an inclusive multilateral world of both regions and global alliances held together by common values, shared norms, and standards, cooperating to meet global challenges, deliver global public goods, harness the potential of new technology, and lay the foundations of a recovery and future prosperity that improves the quality of life and security for all.

There are several lessons from my experience as the Executive Director of UNIFEM, which showed how multilateralism was effectively used in bringing about transformative change during pivotal moments in human history. By its nature, the UN is a hierarchical intergovernmental organization where governments make decisions that affect its directions and functioning. At the same time, the UN has a strong history of mobilization and partnership based on the values and moral authority of the UN Charter. It has opened new possibilities, created spaces, and built alliances to create a people-centred multilateralism that brought about social change and accountability, especially with women and civil society. Central to all our UN work after the fall of the Berlin Wall was the importance of 'inside-outside' partnerships. The UN platform allowed us to work with member states on difficult and sensitive issues like state accountability for ending VAW, and with the Security Council on women, peace, and security. Our success was knowing how to reclaim the convening power and authority of the UN, mobilize the power of constituencies, and use top-down and bottom-up leadership to change the rules of the game when it did not work for women. In short, women, civil society, and governments have the experience of cooperating to build an inclusive multilateralism from the ground up, mobilizing to establish new norms and agendas based on the UN charter as 'We the Peoples' envision the world anew.

From my time at UNIFEM and working with women on the ground and globally, I have learned many dimensions of leadership for transformation, as many women have struggled individually and collectively to change themselves and their world. If we are serious about 'transforming our world', there is much to learn from the best of women's practices about the ways in which power is wielded and how people are empowered to create the possible, using the multilateral system as the global guardian of our shared values to advance shared goals while remaining rooted in their local realities.

First, there is no transformation without empowerment and agency. Women have transformed the context of their lives by becoming the agents of change. The realities of women's daily lives create a textured and intricate understanding of what needs to change. People have dreams and aspirations and, if empowered, can become co-creators of a better future, even in the most precarious circumstances. This, however, requires a governance system that values citizen's participation and engagement. Second, many women have rejected patriarchal power with its 'authority to control' and redefine power as the ability to create and change. Several women leaders have strived for accountable leadership that uses 'power with' and 'power within'—power that does not deprive others but instead grows and multiplies as it is shared. This kind of leadership is an important bedrock to develop trust, a genuine sense of community, and 'the whole of society approach' to engage in the full spectrum of dialogue, cooperation, and action to ensure peace, security and equitable opportunities and live within sustainable eco-boundaries. Third, have the courage to imagine a different world and find ways to create it through collective action based on mutual respect, understanding that people have the freedom to find their own paths and balance the personal and the collective. Fourth, women activist leaders know that the personal is political and the political has to be made personal to make a difference. There is much to learn from women's stories and life histories used to dismantle discrimination and identities constructed by others. Female pioneers, across generations, have created social capital by building trusted networks of alliances, listening and valuing the voice and participation of all who are interested to engage. Finally, we need to be fearless in renewing our world using the universal ethics and values as envisioned in the UN Charter, practising and integrating them into our daily life and decision-making in families, institutions, economies, and societies.

As I reflect on my own story, what endures is the power of the human spirit, individually and collectively, to transcend, reimagine, and rejuvenate. It is a story of living fearlessly in the imperfect world we inherit—summoning the courage to believe that different realities are possible even in the face of immense adversity—living purposefully and taking risks to create change and make the world what it can be. There is no way to know what life will ask of us. Each of us have our unique struggles and sources of inspiration and happiness. The chaos of my childhood forced me to learn that I had to be stronger and braver than most children of my age, and I had to do it as a girl of mixed heritage. I found ways to bounce back even when badly bruised, make real friends, find community, treasure every opportunity to educate and transform myself into a centred human being, find the power within, and do what I know is right. I have journeyed through life experiencing its contradictions and conflicts, the wounds it inflicted, but also the grace and beauty it bestowed. Throughout my life, I was not afraid to make hard decisions and walk away from social expectations and definitions of security and success, of roles and relationships that did not work for me. I have been inspired by idealism and resilience and the legacy of courage of so many. This has ignited a fire within me to hold myself to a high standard of empathy, listen to women who have been pushed into the shadows and the margins, speak my truth, and seek only what I value as a healthy counterbalance to the dysfunction I saw around me.

I am sure that anyone looking at my childhood could not have imagined how my life would unfold and the person I would become. This was only possible because I have been blessed with enlightened mentors, with understanding and love, and deep nourishing relationships with family and friends. It has been a rare privilege to be entrusted with the leadership of two UN organizations at pivotal moments in their history, to be able to use the power of multilateralism to generate ecosystems of hope to bring about a world I would like my daughters and their generation to inherit. My life has been profoundly enriched by Yew Teng and our daughters. Yew Teng lost his battle to cancer a decade ago, but his indomitable spirit and our vows of love are always with me as I watch our daughters become confident, creative, and caring women living phenomenal lives of their own choosing.

As I watch many sunsets and moonrises, as each day turns to night only to reemerge as the dawn, my mind wanders at times to the last days of being with my mother. If I could speak to her once more, I would say to her, 'Mother, don't cry. There is a light that survives the darkest night. I have reached beyond storms and stars to build a life on a horizon of dreams.'

Afterword

Tommy Koh

I thank my good friend, Noeleen Heyzer, for giving me the honour of contributing this Afterword to her memoirs.

Noeleen Heyzer's life story is moving and inspiring. Her extraordinary achievements at the UN have improved the lives of women all over the world. Every girl in Singapore, indeed, in the world, should read this book.

What are the three most important lessons I have learnt from this book?

First, that one should never allow adversity in childhood to prevent one from having aspirations. Noeleen had a very difficult childhood of poverty. She experienced the unravelling of her family when her father became jobless and abandoned the family. Her mother took personal responsibility, but the pressures were too much and she died at the age of twenty-six when Noeleen was only six years old. Fortunately, her maternal grandmother, uncle, and aunt eventually provided her with a supportive environment. Noeleen embodies human resilience at its best, overcoming childhood vulnerabilities to build a highly successful and purpose-driven life. She did very well at school and, through success in education, broke through the barriers of poverty and disadvantage to become a trailblazer of women's global leadership at the UN.

Second, Noeleen is a woman of courage. She takes risks to renew complex institutions and respond to the challenges of the time. When she was appointed the Executive Director of the UNIFEM in 1994, she found, on arrival in New York, that the organization had a major financial crisis. The head of the UNDP offered her a deal—for an annual contribution of $10 million, UNIFEM would agree to be absorbed into UNDP. Noeleen rejected the offer, as she believed that UNIFEM should remain independent. She was confident that if UNIFEM was able to do meaningful work, it would be able to attract political and financial support from governments and foundations. She was proven right. At the end of her tenure, UNIFEM was a powerhouse working on gender equality in the UN with an annual budget of $150 million. The lesson is not to accept the soft option but to have the courage and tenacity to fight for what is right.

Third, this book is about the importance of collaborative leadership to address difficult issues and create new possibilities. The mobilization of women leaders and networks globally raised the issue of VAW at the UN and persuaded the UN General Assembly to adopt a Declaration on the Elimination of Violence against Women. Subsequently, Noeleen worked with the General Assembly to establish a United Nations Trust Fund in Support of Actions to Eliminate Violence against Women in 1996. She experienced an epiphany when she heard the stories of the Tutsi women of Rwanda who were raped during the genocide and the stories of women who were raped during the wars in the Balkans. Together with other women leaders she worked towards an international legal framework that regards sexual violence as a war crime. After a year of hard work, persuading the fifteen members of the UN Security Council, Noeleen and her team had a breakthrough. On 31 October 2000, the Security Council adopted the landmark resolution, 1325, on women, peace, and security. The protection of women and girls in armed conflict has become an important principle of international humanitarian law.

Noeleen Heyzer is both an intellectual and a woman of action. She has made this world a safer and better place for women and girls everywhere. Noeleen Heyzer is truly an inspiring Singaporean. She is a beacon in our troubled world.

Professor Tommy Koh
Singapore's Ambassador to the United Nations
(1968–71; 1974–84)
Chairman, Main Committee of the UN
Conference on Environment and Development
President, Third UN Conference on the Law of the Sea

Acknowledgement

My grateful thanks to the Lee Kong Chian Fund for Excellence for the support to write this book as a Lee Kong Chian Distinguished Fellow at the School of Social Sciences, Singapore Management University.

My deep appreciation to Professor Lily Kong, president of the Singapore Management University for encouraging me to share with the younger generation my leadership experiences at the UN in managing complex institutions to make a positive difference in our multilateral world.

My special thanks to Professor Amartya Sen and Sir Richard Jolly, for graciously agreeing to write the forewords to this book, and to Professor Tommy Koh for his insightful afterword.

Heartfelt thanks to my daughters, Pauline and Lilianne, who urged me to write my life story in a way that would capture the imagination of their generation. They were a constant source of inspiration and emotional support throughout the process of writing, and were my trusted editors for this book.

I am deeply grateful to my team at UNIFEM and to our partners. Their support gave me the courage to be bold and unafraid in leading the organization, transforming structures of discrimination in the midst of our evolving historical and geopolitical landscape. I thank Joanne Sandler, my deputy of many years, for being my soulmate in UNIFEM, and for her comments on the initial draft of the manuscript.

I appreciate my staff at ESCAP who worked so hard to ensure that we were 'fit for purpose', supporting member states to deliver an inclusive and sustainable development agenda for people in the region.

My gratitude to Ambassador Ong Keng Yong for supporting my work on women, peace, and security and non-traditional security issues in ASEAN as a Visiting Distinguished Fellow at the S Rajaratnam School of International Studies, Nanyang Technological University.

My family has been a pillar of strength in good times and bad. Deepest gratitude goes to Uncle Paul for his loving generosity and care when I needed it most, to Aunty Lily, and Grandma for their protection and support at the hardest of times, and to Aunty Anne who was always there for me with her spiritual and practical guidance.

My loving thanks, always, to Yew Teng who pushed me to the edge and encouraged me to 'remember your humanity, forget the rest'. This became the foundation upon which we built our family.

I have been blessed and nourished by so many people throughout my journey. It is not possible to name and thank all of them individually. Many are reflected in the pages of this book but many more are not. Without them there would have been no story.

I have been inspired by the efforts of thousands of women and men who have dedicated their lives to the greater good, including those who wrote the UN Charter out of the ashes of the Second World War and United all Nations to agree to the ground rules for our shared destiny. I thank them for infusing new energy and wisdom into our world, my life, and the lives of so many. We have held together across time, striving to cocreate a greater humanity.

Noeleen Heyzer

Glossary

ADB	Asian Development Bank
AFWIC	African Women in Crisis Countries
AHTF	ASEAN Humanitarian Task Force
APCWD	United Nations Asia and Pacific Centre for Women and Development
APDC	Asian and Pacific Development Centre
APWLD	Asia Pacific Forum on Women, Law and Development
ASEAN	Association of Southeast Asian Nations
BPA	Beijing Platform for Action
CEDAW	Convention on Elimination of All Forms of Discrimination against Women
CRC	United Nations Convention on the Rights of the Child
DAW	Division for the Advancement of Women
DAWN	Development Alternatives for Women in the New Era
DDR	Disarmament, Demobilization and Reintegration
DFID	Department for International Development, United Kingdom
ECOSOC	United Nations Economic and Social Council

ESCAP	Economic and Social Commission for Asia and the Pacific
FWCW	United Nations Fourth World Conference on Women
ICTR	International Criminal Tribunal for Rwanda
IDS	Institute of Development Studies
ILO	International Labour Organization
INSTRAW	International Research and Training Institute for the Advancement of Women
IWC	International Women's Commission
JICA	Japan International Cooperation Agency
MIT	Massachusetts Institute of Technology
NGO	Non-governmental Organization
PONJA	Post-Nargis Joint Assessment
PONREPP	Post-Nargis Recovery and Preparedness Plan
RC	Resident Coordinator
RCEP	Regional Comprehensive Economic Partnership
SCR 1325	Security Council Resolution on Women, Peace and Security 1325
SRSG	Special Representative of the Secretary General
TCG	Tripartite Core Group
UNDAF	United Nations Development Assistance Framework
UNDP	United Nations Development Programme
UNFCCC	United Nations Framework Convention on Climate Change
UNFPA	United Nations Fund for Population Affairs
UNICEF	United Nations Children's Fund
UNIFEM	United Nations Development Fund for Women
VAW	Violence against Women
WHO	World Health Organization